naked jane bares all

a tale of triumph, travails & ta-tas

by Jane Schwartzberg
& Marcy Tolkoff Levy

Library of Congress Cataloging-in-Publication Data
Schwartzberg, Jane and Tolkoff Levy, Marcy
Naked Jane Bares All:
A Tale of Triumph, Travails & Ta-Tas

Cover photo of Jane Schwartzberg by Robert X. Fogarty
of Dear World, reprinted with permission

Cover design by Zanne Papageorgantis

Dedication

For Mickey, Ally, Jack
Mom, Dad
Sue, Len, David
Ben, Max, Gabe and Dash

With love,
Jane

.   .   .

For Mitchell, Daniel
Mom, Dad, Robin, Harry, Melanie, Michael
and those who taught me about courage and fortitude,
Grandma and Michele

With love,
Marcy

Table of Contents

Acknowledgment

Without you, Anita Sands, this book doesn't exist. If, as the Irish proverb says, "Two shorten the road," then just look at what three have done.

Practically from the onset of our meeting, we fused as if we'd known each other forever. What brought and has held us together goes far deeper than anything that could have differentiated us. We found a common conscience and clarity, much stronger than clan or country.

Our amity has been a lesson in unconditional acceptance and the power of honesty. For your foresight, your wisdom, your kind heart and boundless friendship, we are so very grateful.

Jane and Marcy

A very special thank you to Alison Jones and Geralda Sotolongo for their contributions to our "book club."

Prologue

In many ways, I've led the life of an average Jane. Certainly, there have been some moments of glory in my life as well. For example, I graduated from college with honors—and then there was that Internet start-up I launched. But best of all, at the age of 31, was falling in love with and marrying the most wonderful man in the world. There was all the excitement one might expect of a new bride. A few months later, I got cancer. Never again would I be an average Jane.

Fast-forward 10 years, and the doctors told me I was cured. A wife and mother of two, I had a good job and a lovely home in the suburbs of New Jersey.

But the doctors were wrong. It turned out that the cancer had been with me all along. Most people will live their entire lives without ever hearing a surgeon say: "Our worst fears have been confirmed. You have cancer and it's all over your chest wall and lungs."

So when I heard those words, my reaction was anything but ordinary. It started in my toes. It was as if my entire body were erupting, relinquishing, surrendering. Every droplet of food, bile, glucose, water and gaseous remnant of anesthesia shifted and whatever was in me that wasn't tied down seemed to bubble to the surface in a tsunami of revulsion. It all lurched forward, my muscles twitching and contorting, as if my body were turning itself inside out.

My lunch spewed forth from my throat and ended in an unceremonious splat—all over the surgeon's stunning pair of $400 Tory Burch pumps. A symbolic "Take that."

I lost hope, security and peace of mind, along with any semblance of control I had deluded myself into thinking I possessed.

It was all gone. I was empty. That's when I free-fell into the abyss.

Today, the picture of my life appears tidy. Like the used car on a dealership lot that's been in a flood, you can't see that anything's amiss from the outside.

You cannot tell that my insides have been tossed like a salad and are held together by a mesh band and metal staples. Many aspects of my life are still ordinary, average, even mundane. But I think you will agree that, in some ways, my life thus far has been *extra*ordinary.

I fight to maintain my place in the world and keep reminding myself that I matter. I must.

I am Naked Jane and this is my story.

The big reveal

I was home alone one evening in February of 2000. Mickey, my husband of three months, was out. While chatting away on the phone, I was absentmindedly fingering the V-neck collar of my pajama top. I felt something hard, like a small marble, in my right breast.

I was 31 years old, running a start-up software company and planning to leave in a few days for a big work trip. I thought a doctor would laugh at me for coming in to have it checked.

But Mick made me promise to get it looked at right away, so I squeezed in an appointment with the local breast center.

The doctor shut her eyes tightly as she examined my chest. Then she excused herself and left the room for what seemed like a long time. I was annoyed because I needed to go home so I could get ready for my trip. Sitting there in an orange and red seersucker robe much nicer than what I would come to know at the hospitals, I did not think for one second that I could be sick. In fact, I don't think I'd ever felt better.

The doctor returned to do an ultrasound of my breast. She squinted as she looked at the screen. "I really have to run," I told her. "I'm on my way to Arkansas for a business trip. I need to get home to pack." She didn't answer.

"No, really, I appreciate your being very thorough, but I have to go." More silence and looking at the screen.

She put down the equipment she was using, leaned in close and took my hand. "I'm sorry, Jane. I am quite certain you have cancer."

"What the fuck did she say?" I asked myself.

Five days later, I was in the hospital having a bilateral mastectomy and 30 lymph nodes removed from under my right arm to check for spreading. I could have opted for a single mastectomy, but figured, "Let's just be done with it and then I won't have to worry."

I was given the choice of two types of reconstruction. The first was implants. They explained that once my breasts were taken off, tissue expanders would be put in under some chest muscles. The expanders would be injected with saline over a few months to stretch the muscle. Later, the expanders would be removed and permanent implants close to the size of my natural breasts would be inserted. An image flashed across my mind of me as an old lady with a saggy body but round, perky, never-to-droop breasts.

The other choice I was given was called an abdominal tram flap. To be a candidate for this surgery, I needed to have enough fat in my belly to create brand new breasts. I never thought I'd be happy to be told that I had "plenty of fat to work with." My doctor explained that the procedure would be painful, but the results were quite good.

After my breasts were surgically removed, I would be cut from hip to hip. My abdominal muscles would be pushed up to where my breasts were, and the fat from my belly would be used to fill in the new breasts. I could not

imagine the technicalities of the surgery, and did
not really want to. After the doctor told me that
implants last only a certain number of years and
would eventually need to be surgically changed,
I decided that the tram was the way to go.

During the six-hour operation, there were some
30 friends and relatives in the waiting room—or
so I was told. All of them had danced at my
wedding just weeks earlier. Now they waited as
my breasts were being taken off. They waited
and, as they had done at the wedding, they ate.

In my family, we eat when we're happy, when
we're sad, when we're nervous. Someone had
brought in platters of sandwiches, because G-d
forbid someone should starve. I wonder how
many other women have their mastectomies
catered.

As it turned out, the doctor's description
"painful" was an understatement. In fact, had I
fully comprehended the degree of physical pain I
would experience as a result of the tram flap, I
doubt I would have signed up for it. My body
was opened up and put back together like a
tight drum. I could not walk, lift my legs or get

up to use the bathroom for several days. I had drainage tubes passing through my chest and abdomen, with clear bulbs at the end of them to collect whatever was coming out of the surgical sites. My body was meticulously wrapped so that I could not see what was left behind.

It wasn't until many days later, when I was recovering at my parents' house, that I told my mom I needed to see. She did not encourage me, nor did she tell me not to, but asked me how I wanted to do it. I had her undress me and unwrap the bandages as I stood several feet from the full-length mirror in the room I'd slept in as a little girl.

We faced each other, with the mirror behind her, blocking me from seeing my naked body. I asked her to move a tiny bit over so I could start to see my incisions and skin. The sight of all the cuts and bruising was dizzying. We stood quietly for a while. Then I told her to move over another few inches. When she did, I could see that I no longer had any nipples, and they had been replaced with disks of skin from my abdomen.

After a few more moves, my mom stood next to me as I gazed at my reconstructed body; in my mind, it was cut everywhere. I could not quite understand whose body it was. When I noticed that a birthmark I'd had on my stomach was now on one of the puzzle pieces of skin that formed my breasts, she had to hold me up.

1 B.C.

I feel lucky in countless ways. First on my list of things that make me feel lucky is being born to my parents. A close second is meeting and marrying my life partner, Mick. Of course, we argue just like any couple. I mean, just because we've looked death square in the face together doesn't mean that we are all of a sudden going to stop annoying each other. But he is a first-class, loving and very handsome guy I am blessed to be sharing my life with.

Finding him was not so easy. I went on more dates than I care to remember. On one that I sometimes still smile about, the guy spent all of dinner telling me how wealthy he was. When it came time to pay, he asked me for 18 bucks.

In protest against the enormous amount of work it was to get ready, I stopped investing the time in a hair wash, blow-out and leg shave before first dates. So I went with my hair dirty and quickly clipped back to meet Mick. We were introduced through mutual friends and I liked him immediately. He had an air of calm about him that was very appealing. I assumed, given our engaging conversation and the easy flow of things, that he liked me, too. Apparently, that was not at all the case. I'll let him explain.

There was absolutely no chemistry the first time I met Jane.

I saw her as she was coming down the staircase in her apartment building. The lighting was poor and she did not look great. I mean, she looked fine. But it was definitely not love at first sight.

We went to a Thai restaurant on our first date. I'd had a lot of dating experience and was gauging how much give-and-take there was. She definitely did more talking than I did.

Being a nice guy and not wanting to say "I probably won't call you," I told her I would call. Well, maybe I would, I thought to myself. More likely not. Said I would. Just to wrap it up. Pretty sure I wouldn't.

But I had nothing else going on. No other prospects. So after about a week, I called her. We went out on a second date to Ellis Island. It was fun, but there really wasn't much chemistry then either, at least not for most of the time we spent together.

After Ellis Island, we went out to dinner, and I felt we were warming to one another. I sure was warming to her. She was feisty but really sweet and she made me laugh. When she left to go to the ladies' room, I found myself missing her. A lot.

After just a few weeks of constantly being together, we both knew this was "it." We were in mad love with one another. That's all that we knew. For about three months, we were inseparable; three months later, we were engaged; six months later, we were married in an intimate wedding with 350 of our nearest and dearest friends and relatives.

There was no formal wedding party. My two best friends and Jane's sister, Sue, made a beautiful toast. Her family is part of this big, close Cuban-Jewish community. We danced on a conga line, shaking maracas. Some guests held up baby pictures of Janie and me. Luis, my new father-in-law, sang the Seven Blessings. Janie's friend June sang too. It was joyous and rich with culture and love and warmth. I was home.

.　.　.

See? I told you that Mick had a different take. But it doesn't matter. He married me—twice.

Around the time of our first wedding anniversary, a few months after I finished chemo, I effectively gave him permission to find someone who wasn't sick and could see him into old age. "We don't have children yet," I told him. "I'm giving you a pass. A get-out-of-jail-free card."

He didn't hesitate: "Not only am I not going anywhere, but I'd marry you all over again."

And he did. Mick made all the plans. He invited two couples and made arrangements to get re-hitched at the Little White Wedding chapel in—where else?—Las Vegas. We bought the $40 Drive-Thru Special package, which featured an Elvis impersonator. Turns out we were in very good company. The Little White Wedding Chapel featured prominently in at least one of the marriages of celebrities like Frank Sinatra, Bruce Willis and Michael Jordan.

We renewed our vows while sitting in a 1959 Cadillac convertible. Murals overhead featured the sayings, "Our marriage was made in heaven" and "I can't live without you." The package came with photographs, a VCR recording of the ceremony and a "Rules for a Happy Marriage" booklet.

The priest spoke about the beauty of two hearts beating as one and married our Jewish selves "in the name of Jesus Christ." It didn't matter who married us or where we were. All that mattered was that it was us, our dear friends— and Elvis.

Preaching to the choir

During the summer of 2011, if anyone had asked me if I believed in a higher power, I would have said that I wasn't sure. I honestly couldn't say what I was sure of or in whom I believed. Except love. I believed in the power of love. Plain and simple.

When my rabbi asked if I would be interested in addressing our congregation, I didn't hesitate to say "yes," thinking I could say something that would help someone sitting in temple that Saturday morning at Sabbath services. Maybe sharing my despair would help lessen someone else's.

As for what I would say, well, that proved to be a more difficult decision. Over the course of the next few months, especially in the middle of the night when I couldn't sleep, I sat at the computer and typed. I wrote and rewrote frantically up until the night before I spoke in March of 2012.

After a family friend and fellow temple member introduced me to the congregation, I walked up to the podium, took a deep breath and began to address the many faces that filled the seats, including my relatives and friends …

Shabbat Shalom. My name is Jane Schwartzberg. I'm a 43-year-old wife, daughter, sister, aunt, friend and mother of two children, ages six and eight.

I'd like to share my story, with three goals in mind. First, I want to convey how enormous and powerful our acts of kindness and tikkun olam (which means repairing the world) can be. I know this for sure as I gratefully have been on the receiving end of so many and am able to stand here in front of you largely thanks to them.

Second, I want to give you some practical advice on what may be helpful to someone going through a situation similar to mine. I know everyone needs different things, so I speak to you knowing only what helped me; I certainly don't know what works for everyone. And last, I want to thank you for helping to hold me and my family up over these past years.

In 2000, a few months after marrying my husband Mickey, I was diagnosed with a curable form of breast cancer. I fought aggressively with the entire medical arsenal offered to me and with the love and support of an army of people. My parents have always taught me that with thoughtfulness and lots of hard work, I could accomplish anything. So, I believed that if I did all the right things medically, held out lots of hope, and took impeccable care of myself physically and mentally, I would be able to beat the cancer, a belief that offered me much comfort.

As anyone who has dealt with this will understand, each day I found my grounding again. I racked up good appointments, clean scans and some distance from the trauma. I never again felt the solid grounding I had imagined I stood on before getting sick, but it was sufficient. I did not want to wish time away, but sometimes it was hard not to. The further away I got from my treatments, the more hopeful my loved ones and I felt. Days turned into months and months became years until Mickey and I felt optimistic enough to try to conceive. We went on to have a daughter, Ally, and a son, Jack.

Life rolled along, as it always does, no matter what. In the spring of 2010, a decade after my initial diagnosis, my oncologist uttered the words I longed to hear. "You're cured," he said. I'd had 10-plus years of being normal. Blood, tumor markers, scans—everything was normal. Except it wasn't.

A year later, in April of 2011, I went from "cured" to "incurable." I learned that I still had cancer and that, in fact, it had spread. It turned out that for all those years, cancer had been my "constant companion" and it will continue to be for as long as I am here. This time, although treatable, it's incurable. This time, I'm the mother of two beautiful children. This time, my heart broke irreparably.

I felt like I'd disappointed all the people with cancer others had sent my way so I could inspire them, to whom my existence had said, "I got better and you will, too." Now, I could no longer be a symbol of hope.

I quickly had to learn how to let myself "fall" really, really hard and, at the same time, to open myself up to the outrageous amount of support that you and the universe have offered me. I include every one of you in this. Even if you didn't directly support me, you've helped to sustain a community that has.

By "fall," I mean letting go of my desire or need to control things and accepting my medical and physical reality. It also means surrendering to the part of my life and health over which I am helpless. It is not "giving up"—instead, it is collapsing into the humbling reality that so much is out of my hands. There is a peace that comes along with this.

I mention this because only when I was able to really let myself fall could I accept help and then start to try to get up again. By opening myself up, I have learned to stop apologizing for needing so much help and to accept it graciously. I needed you to show up for me and my family and you did— over and over and over again.

In fact, I didn't even know it, but for many years you helped me prepare for my life after I felt not just bent, but broken. You did this simply by being present in your own life, with all its many challenges. You too have experienced grief and despair, in different forms, for many reasons. You struggled for your own and your loved ones' physical, mental and spiritual health. You lost parents, partners, brothers and sisters, best friends and even children.

And your loss always came too soon. Like me, you felt broken, from disappointment or heartbreak, or simply from life not being what you had wished and imagined. At times, you fought for your life to turn out differently, but to no avail.

And when the fight was over, you grieved heavily and for as long as you needed to, and then you soldiered on. In letting me see you do that, you helped me. You showed me that it could be done; and you made me understand that no matter how long I will be here, whether for days or decades more, my loved ones will always figure out how to go on, just as many of you have. This is a tremendous comfort to me.

And, more recently and deliberately, you showed up in countless other ways. Over these past months, you have fed us, literally and spiritually.

You took our children into your homes for play dates and care. You drove us to tests and medical appointments and sat for endless hours with us in hospitals. You spoke on my behalf to doctors, to colleagues, to people who wanted to know how I was doing. You filled in my disability papers and transported my medical records when we could no longer handle another task.

You told us and showed us that no matter what happened, my family and I would not be alone. You included me in meditations and prayers of all different faiths and with people across the globe. Your presence and voice right here gave strength to the prayers uttered for me and so many others in need of healing. And when you prayed for me, you called me by my name and held in your mind an image of me strong and healthy.

You helped me to get good care in hospitals and in operating rooms, when my feelings of vulnerability were at a peak. When I was certain I would never again have a career after being so ill for so long, you said loudly and clearly "We still value you and we will welcome your contribution when you're ready to give one." You helped me fight to regain my self-esteem and a post-illness place for myself.

After the fridge was filled with food and the kids were dropped off, after we were back from medical appointments and had scheduled the next ones, after the prescriptions were filled and the e-mails sent, you sat with us, quietly. You let the silence speak for itself. You understood that one of the most powerful things you could do to support me was to do absolutely nothing but exist with me in my utter fear and uncertainty.

I'm often asked "What can I do to help?" Again, I can speak only for myself and I know that everyone's list is different, but for me, when I'm struggling, let me suggest: Be in my life at my pace, let me take the lead, make your presence, availability and support known, but do it without any expectations or requirements for a response.

Many people in a similar place find empowerment☐ —not me; I am simply exhausted. With your help, Mickey and I and the rest of my family have once again started stringing days together. We live what Mickey has named our "new normal."

As we go from scan to scan and from one medical appointment to the next, we carry every single act of love and kindness you've shown us in our hearts. Because of these acts, we are often able to be present and available to our children, our other loved ones, our jobs and our communities.

What you have done for us has dramatically and positively impacted the course of our lives. In turn, it has affected every person with whom we come into contact. I hope you understand why I think your willingness to perform acts of kindness toward my family and people like me is one of the most powerful tools we possess.

I started out by saying I wanted to do three things this morning. I wanted to convey how impactful our acts of kindness can be. I hope I have. I wanted to offer some practical guidance on supporting someone going through a challenge like mine. I hope I've done that too.

Finally, I wanted to thank you. Let me say that I can't possibly take in all you've done for us because it's more goodness than I can process. I am just stunned at the stamina that you have shown to offer support to me and others in need.

You comfort and inspire me. Thank you for the abundance you have given me.

Red devil

The poison—I mean the cure—almost did me in.

Chemotherapy started about six weeks after my mastectomy and abdominal tram flap. Every three weeks for four months, I would sit there for several hours while they piped "red devil" into my bloodstream, so named for its deep red color and high levels of toxicity. The drug is designed, of course, to kill the cancer cells—as well as who knows what else.

I have never experienced headaches like I did after treatment. My head felt as if it would explode. I'd lie in bed for hours, hold my head and rock.

If I could have been paid for puking, I would have zillions of dollars. It was particularly painful because I'd been freshly sliced and diced. I was afraid that throwing up would make the stitching that held my insides together come loose, causing my core to burst like a smashed baseball. Instinctively, when I heaved, I placed my hands firmly on the front of my body, pressing against the mesh band that stretched from my pelvis to my chest.

Each day was a roulette wheel of suffering. Round and round the ball would go and which symptom would appear, I did not know.

At the time, the expression "chemo brain" was not a commonly used phrase—even among the cancer population. Yet even without knowing the term, I was certain my brain was being affected by the chemicals. I wasn't acting like myself. I kept saying to anyone who would listen, "I can't concentrate. My head's not right. I'm in a bubble." I could see people I'd known for years and not be able to recall their names. I told my oncologist there was something wrong with my brain, but he chalked it up to trauma and stress.

My brain no longer felt familiar to me. A part of me knew it was the chemicals that had messed me up. Another part of me was terrified that I was losing my mind.

After I was first diagnosed and again after the relapse, I let go of caring about stuff like make-up and what I wore. I was certain I would never care about such things again. When you're in a seriously bad place, or a deeply spiritual place, after you've danced with death, you can't focus on these trivial things. Your life is consumed with basics—like trying not to suffer and just getting through each moment, each hour, each day. Ugh. Such heaviness.

For the few months I was bald, I refused to wear a wig. It was my statement to the world: "Yup—here I am." My hair had always been one of my favorite physical attributes so I was happy when it started to grow back in. Even though it grew back gray, I remember initially thinking, "Beautiful."

Clearly, I must have lost my fucking mind. G-d bless the women who feel great with their gorgeous silver hair. I ain't one of 'em.

As much as we may curse the emphasis on appearance and beauty, we live in the world we live in, and part of reengaging with life is caring about the superficial things at least to some extent. It took many months, but little by little, piece by piece, I started looking like my old self— healthy Jane, not cancer Jane.

When I finally called to make an appointment with my colorist, it was a sign that I was ready to dip my toe back into the world again. One day, instead of putting on sweatpants, I put on jeans. Another day, instead of sneakers, I put on sandals. Next, a little blush. And before I knew it, I'd gone from "Who cares?" to "I care. And shit, I look good."

Baby talk

I remember the reconstructive surgeon standing in front of me, marking up my body to delineate where he had to make the cuts. "My doctors are telling me I probably won't be able to have kids, but if I could get pregnant, how would I give birth after all this surgery?" I asked him. "Janie," he said, "I promise you that if you manage to get pregnant, I will find a way to get the baby out of you safely."

After my mastectomy and before chemotherapy, Mick and I learned that the chemotherapy would put me into menopause, maybe permanently. Of course, no one was sure. There was little data about young women having children after chemo.

As a "just in case," we were advised to freeze embryos that could later be implanted. Or we could adopt. So we went to a fertility specialist to talk about our options. After we saw her, we spoke to her staff. All they talked about was how much it cost, the accepted methods of payment and what they would do with our embryos if we didn't pay on time. Brrrrrrr! A brief exchange with a toll booth operator would have been warmer and more personal.

Mick and I sat in silence on the drive home.

When we finally did talk, we decided not to sign up for who-knew-how-many-more months of nonessential doctor and hospital visits, needles and invasive medical procedures, and said "no thank you" to freezing the embryos.

About two years later, I started getting my period again. That was a wonderful surprise, instead of the huge hassle it used to be. We talked about the potential risks of pregnancy. There was some discussion about pregnancy hormones fueling a cancer recurrence, but I got confident clearance from my doctors. When I became pregnant soon afterward, Mick and I were amazed and thrilled beyond words.

I called the reconstructive surgeon and said "A couple of years ago, you made me a promise. Do

you remember what it was?" He replied "Yes, I do."
And then I joyfully told him: "Well, it looks like
you're going to have to take a baby out of me."

It was a neat trick to deliver the baby without
disturbing his handiwork from the tram flap. He
was there in the delivery room with my
obstetrician.

Lying on the operating room table, I watched a
miraculous symphony take place—as the two
doctor-conductors moved in perfect synchronicity,
conferring about where to cut, how much to pull
and how to bring the baby safely into the world. At
the time, it was such an unusual occurrence—
delivering the baby of a woman who was stitched
from neck to navel—that the room was filled with
hospital staff who wanted to observe.

When they pulled our daughter out, the room
erupted with applause. I remember looking at
Ally and thinking, "I can't believe that someone
as physically and emotionally scarred as I am
gave birth to such a healthy, beautiful child."

When I had Jack, the reconstructive surgeon
was there again. Both times, he brought a

medical team with him. Both times, he didn't send a bill.

Ally's arrival in 2003 buoyed my healing and contributed to my feeling "normal," whatever that may mean. By the time Jack was born in 2005, I was well on my way to feeling "whole." The same people who had cheered my family on while we fought the cancer welcomed our children into the world with open arms and so much love. It was humbling, to say the very least, to have support for such disparate aspects of our lives.

Meet the parents

I come from a long line of survivors. My parents were born in Cuba to immigrant families who had settled in Havana—the last stop on a long journey spent outpacing the Nazis.

On my mother's side, my grandmother and great-grandmother were from the Czech Republic and were about to be shipped off to a concentration camp. They escaped by way of the mountains à la *Sound of Music*, settling for a time in France, where my grandparents met. My grandfather had gone from Salonika in Greece to Paris, where he lived as a young man.

Three days before my grandfather was to be picked up by the Nazis in France, he and my grandmother got out and made their way to Spain and then Portugal, a neutral country. They didn't know where they were going, but they knew what they were leaving. From Portugal, they managed to get visas to Cuba. They would have gone anywhere. On the boat trip to Cuba, my grandmother was pregnant with my uncle. When there were attacks on the ship, they had to shut off all the lights. The grueling voyage took three months.

My father's parents were from a small town outside of Bialystok, which at the time was in Poland. They were, as my dad proudly says, *shtetl* Jews. My grandfather, whom we lovingly called Zayde, came to Cuba at the age of 19 and never saw his family again. Three years later, he brought his sweetheart from Poland to Havana and they married. She was our beloved Bubbe.

In Cuba, life was good but it was also hard. My maternal grandfather started out selling wares and fabrics from house to house, eventually growing the business into a successful company. Zayde found work managing a diner that catered to new immigrants. Later, he would have success as a supplier to small shoe manufacturers. The nuclear families were close, but there was no extended family. They remained scared that worshiping openly could be risky, so for many years they practiced their faith cautiously and privately.

Over the years, they became less secretive about being Jewish. My mother was 15 and my father 22 when they met in 1958 at a Jewish Community Center. They fell deeply in love and agreed that they wanted to spend their lives together. About two years later, Castro came into power and the Communists started running Cuba. Government officials went up and down the streets, demanding people give them their names. They even took over private businesses, including both of my grandfathers'.

One Friday afternoon in October of 1960, government officials approached my mother and uncle and began to question them. Having lived through persecution once, my grandparents didn't want to wait to see what would happen. The next Monday morning, they put my mom and uncle on a plane to the United States. She was 16 and he was 17, and my grandparents followed soon afterward. It was a difficult time. In Cuba, they had friends, a home and a business. In America, they were refugees.

At the time the government closed the University of Havana, my father was ranked first in a class of several hundred students at its law school. He told my mother that if she was going to leave, so was he. They took different flights but arrived in the United States on the same day. Bubbe came in 1961 and Zayde, because he had problems with his passport, wasn't able to escape to join his family until a year later.

Unlike my mother, who had attended an American school in Cuba, my father came to this country not knowing how to speak English. At the same time that my mother gave him English lessons, she was sending letters on his behalf to apply to law schools. Replies started coming in. Based on school transcripts and recommendations from his professors in Cuba, Yale Law School accepted him on the condition that he learn English. My mother was a good teacher and, fortunately, my father was a quick study. Five months later, he could speak English.

After Dad finished his first year of law school, my parents got married. That was 1962. My sister, Sue, was born in 1966, I came along in 1968 and my brother, David, arrived 10 years later.

For my entire upbringing, I lived in the house where my parents still live. I even carved my initials and a heart in cement on the sidewalk. And when the sidewalk was recemented many years later, my dad made sure my initials were left untouched.

Legacy

My mother thinks she is partly to blame for my getting cancer. In high school, I gained a lot of weight and developed—well, let's just say it was *extreme adolescence*. My breasts were huge and my periods painful, so my mom took me to "the best" doctors, who advised that I start taking hormones.

We have sometimes wondered if this was the catalyst that ultimately led to the cancer. It's natural, I suppose, to want to try and find a reason, a cause. Makes us feel that there's a rhyme and reason to the order of the universe. For me, I ask, what does it matter?

I choose not to spend time wondering how or why I got sick. It feels like a waste of time and is irrelevant, really. I'd rather focus on the fight, on what I can control. We all have a flame, and it's not always strong. So we have to figure out how to fan it.

It can't be my story that I'm in the ground at 33 or 43. It can't be that my family brought us here—worked so hard and struggled to give us a good life—for me to be sick and die so young. At least that is what I tell myself. This motivates me to keep fighting. It helps me keep my dukes up, long after my arms are bone-tired.

My family's stories infused me as I was growing up. I always aimed for excellence, mostly to prove that I was worthy. And how do you do that? You honor the storytellers.

I wanted to show them that I was worthy of the opportunities they had worked so hard to give me. I always thought I could prove that I was deserving by working hard and not taking anything for granted.

The cancer thing puts a different spin on being worthy. They fought for their place. Now I fight for mine. And the fight is not just about getting through being cut, burned or hooked up to a machine. It's also a fight to show up and be present in my days.

But we do whatever we need to do, right?
I believe we have the responsibility to do
anything we can to be present for the ones
who love and need us. That's what my parents,
my grandparents and my great-grandparents
did. To give up would be to say that all their
struggles did not matter. I cannot—*I will not*—
let that happen.

I do windows

I wouldn't exactly say that I *chose* to stop working.
It was more like I was beaten into submission. I
intended to work through my pregnancy with Ally,
but my body would have nothing to do with it. As
Ally grew in my belly, so did the pain. The plastic
mesh holding me together clearly was not
designed to accommodate a baby. Even after Ally
was born, my reconstructed body had a hard time
recovering from infections related to the cesarean
section. It was so challenging that two years later,
when I got pregnant again with Jack, several of
my friends asked me if I had lost my mind.

Despite my best intentions of being engaged
professionally and contributing financially to
our family, my career came to a screeching halt.
And it stayed there for many years. I think it
was a combination of fatigue, my wanting to be
home with our little beauties, and my inability to
have my teeth brushed before 11:00 a.m. that
resulted in my job falling way down on the list of

priorities. I figured I would be out of work for at least several months. I blinked, and over seven years went by.

If you think it's hard to climb Mount Everest or to complete a marathon, try getting a job after you have spent seven years wiping butts, taking long walks and looking for the best price on organic apples. Although I had enjoyed my time on Wall Street and building start-up companies, when people asked me what I wanted to do professionally, I would look at them quizzically and say "I'm not sure." Worse, when they asked me what I was good at, I would have to pause and think really hard. I truly had no idea.

What I could remember was the feeling of satisfaction I had when I was working outside the home. I don't regret a moment of my time as a full-time mother. It certainly is the hardest job I have ever held and the one I am by far the most proud of. But I felt ready and wanted to go back to my career. I knew that doing so would really help me to feel like my old self, which I desperately wanted.

It was going to take a miracle—or in my case, my friend Mary Ann—to make something happen. Because she is so damn smart, she understood that the only way someone would hire me would be through a really good recommendation from a trusted friend and colleague. And she was prepared to give one. She reached out to Brian, who she knew was the one Wall Street person on the planet who would understand the complicated circumstances of my professional life. Within weeks, I was sitting in a small conference room being asked to tell him about myself.

Just as Mary Ann had said, Brian was magical. He had achieved outrageous professional success in a tough and competitive industry, and still was kind and spoke with tremendous humility. I knew immediately that I would follow him into a fire if he needed me to.

"What do you want to do?" he asked me. I had thought about this long and hard. I replied, "I want to be part of a great team building a business. I will vacuum the floors, dust the paintings and water the plants, if that is the best use of my time. I want to work, and if I'm part of a team I believe in, I'm game for anything."

After many more meetings over the course of several months, I was offered a job and accepted it with both tremendous excitement and trepidation.

Aside from the suit I'd bought for the interviews, every outfit I owned had huge shoulder pads, which had been out of style for years. I spent several months of savings on clothes that would help me look as if I belonged in an office. Not to mention the make-up, the shoes, even some earrings—I needed to get everything. And I did.

It took a while, but I got the hang of all of it. Now I can even navigate the dizzying corporate cafeteria and the maze of training rooms. I am confident that I am doing what I said I wanted to do. I am contributing to the success of my team, and I feel so proud of that. Now, just like everyone else, I walk around checking my BlackBerry, peppering my dialogue with corporate speak and a more-than-occasional acronym. I fit right in.

Phantom body

It took me a long time to accept what was, to make peace with what my body had become. I sought to view my body as "working well" despite serious challenges, and to honor it for that.

I struggled to make some sense of it all and to resign myself to the reality. It was not easy. How do you accept losing body parts? How do you make peace with your body when it feels so much older than it really is? How do you inhabit a body that is yours but feels foreign to you?

One morning, I got out of the shower and saw blood on the floor. I could not figure out where the blood was coming from. I looked at the front and back of my hands. Then I checked my nose in the mirror. Nothing. It turned out that I had scraped one of my reconstructed breasts on the side of the shower door. Since I have no feeling there, I couldn't feel the torn skin.

I was angry for having parts of my body that existed cosmetically only, but also grateful for being able to "pass" as a whole person. To see me in the street, you'd think I look quite normal. But I know that my physical body has been slashed. I know that I'll never again have full use of my right arm, because of complications that developed after so many lymph nodes were removed.

Once, when I was at a dinner party for a friend's birthday, one of the other guests—a very attractive, petite woman—was talking about her new, surgically enhanced boobs. All of the women got up from the table and followed her into the bathroom for a peek at her chest. I went, too, because that's what all the women were doing.

They *ooohed* and *aaahed* over her perfectly round and perky breasts, laughing as they examined her carefully. When they left the bathroom, I stayed behind and vomited. I wondered what these women would say if they saw the mess that was my body.

I try not to tolerate a high level of concern and scrutiny over physical appearances. But I live in this world, too. Every woman, including me, deserves to feel that she is attractive. Instead, I am a scarred imposter. I have nightmares that someone will reveal my true identity.

In one of them, I'm trying on an outfit in a dressing room and people whip open the curtain. They stand there, horrified, because they can see that my breasts are fake and that my body was ripped apart and stitched back together. I am terrified of being discovered, terrified of people seeing me for what I really am.

Radio silence

When I was in business school, I relayed my little pipe dream of becoming a talk show host to one of our lecturers. He told me that if I pursued my dream, he'd support a project on media personalities and the entertainment industry. At dinner with him and a few friends, I formalized our agreement by signing the back of the dinner receipt with "I promise to give my dream breathing space." And that's how my campus radio show was born. After too many drinks that night, a classmate came up with the name *Bare It All With Naked Jane*, to reflect the no-holds-barred conversations I would have with my guests.

I was determined to be different from the plethora of talk show hosts on the air—often male, mean and narrow-minded. My first guest was a gay auto mechanic who owned his own shop and employed lesbian mechanics. After that, I would move on to workplace diversity, depression, eating disorders and sex toys.

Good evening. Welcome to "Bare it all!" I'm Naked Jane in search of the naked truth, coming to you live from KZSU, Stanford, California, 90.1 on your FM dial.

My guest tonight is Fred Jackson, the spokesman for a local nudist camp. Fred, you've told me that women have experienced major changes in their lives as a result of going to nudist camps. Let's talk about some practical issues: Where in G-d's name do you put your keys?

.   .   .

Jane: Thank you for your willingness to talk openly about HIV and its impact on your life. Did you perceive the test result as a death sentence?

Guest: Not exactly. It was more like "What do I do now? How do I get on with my life right now? What's my next step?"

Jane: Are you scared of dying?

．　　．　　．

Jane: I want to switch gears a little bit and talk about your mastectomy. You write in the book about your unveiling, the unveiling of your bandages following your mastectomy. What was that like?

Guest: I think at the time, I was so afraid I would be squeamish or horrified, and then I saw a little piece at a time and by the time I saw the whole thing, it didn't seem as bad as whatever my worst fears were.

．　　．　　．

Pretty ironic, eh? Well, what was even more ironic was the fact that about 20 years later— not long after being declared "cured"—chatty Naked Jane was suddenly and completely silenced. My voice was gone. I tried to speak, but no sound would come out. I couldn't scream a whisper.

We went to a slew of doctors to figure out what it was. Grabbing at what appeared to be straws, we asked if it could be related to the cancer, but that idea was met with a resounding "No." For months, I believed them when they said I had some kind of infection or bronchitis. At some point, though, I couldn't deny that something was very wrong.

Try not speaking for a day and you'll have an idea of what it was like. It went on for five months. It even hurt to try and speak softly. Moved my lips but nothing came out. I'd yell silently, to no one in particular. Still. No. Voice.

At work, I would write notes to my colleagues on pads and, of course, on the computer. I was afraid I would be fired. Here I was, finally back at work and feeling excited about my professional future, and I couldn't participate verbally in anything. I couldn't tell a soul what I was thinking—at least not when I was thinking it. It was humiliating.

And maddening. I couldn't speak to my kids. Couldn't read a bedtime story aloud. Couldn't tell them I loved them. Couldn't help with homework. Nothing. It was as if the whole world just shut down in silence. I got to the point where I would throw things out of frustration. I would stomp. I was trying to hold on to my sanity for dear life. At night, I'd lie in bed sobbing—without making a sound.

As part of the search for my voice, doctors put me through a litany of tests. They suggested giving me an injection through my throat to fill it with something that might help me get my voice back. The idea was the vocal cords weren't touching each other the way they should, so the injection might fill the space and help me produce sound. I didn't need a voice to make clear my feeling about having a huge needle stuck into my neck.

Soon after this, the doctors told me definitively that the cancer had recurred and spread. My ovaries were removed to reduce my body's production of estrogen, a feeder of the cancer.

About 10 days later, as I was lying on the couch at home recuperating from the surgery, I asked a friend who was visiting "John, my voice, do you hear me?" It just clicked back.

My doctors say it was just a coincidence. That's what they say when they don't know the answer.

What I think happened is that all the crazy cancer inflammation caused an enlarged lymph node in my chest to put pressure on my vocal nerve. So after I had my ovaries removed, the inflammation went down and the node reduced its pressure on the vocal cord. And my voice returned. At least, that's my story and I'm sticking to it.

.   .   .

Jane: Before we get into the specifics of your organization, let's talk generally about the men's movement. Last I checked, men were in pretty good shape in terms of status, power, money-making potential compared to women, so why is there a men's movement?

Guest: I could make the same case for women if I were to pick and choose among the stereotypes and statistics that are convenient.

Jane: Let's take the case where a man is morally against abortion and he impregnates a women and she does not want the child. Do you think a man should have the right to insist that the woman should have the child?

Guest: That's one of the toughest questions you could ask me.

Jane: Then it's a good thing I asked ...

This is Naked Jane signing off. Until tomorrow, stay naked!

Birthright

Everything about my grandfather was big. His body. His voice. Even his sneezes were loud and would shake the house. But biggest of all was his bold and boisterous manner.

He was in the *shmata*, or fabric, business—first in Cuba and then in America, where, after many years, his Fabricville stores became a success in northern New Jersey. I can remember when I was a little girl and he would take me to a rug marketplace where he would haggle with sellers over the price. Grandpa was very sure of himself and took control of every situation.

He'd walk around barking, "How much?" If someone called out "$500," he'd blast them. "*What*? $500? I'll give you $80." And they would proceed to scream at each other. He loved every minute of it. What would often end up happening was something like the seller saying, "We will not take less than $200." Grandpa would hand them $100 and start walking out with the rug. All the while I clung to his pants leg, simultaneously embarrassed and exhilarated.

As I got a little older, I was more often mortified than delighted. He would bargain with the local Montclair shopkeepers, even when there were price tags on the merchandise. One afternoon I went with him to the eyeglass store. When Grandpa picked up a pair of glasses from the display, the owner immediately said "Mr. Tiano, I paid $60 for those. I can't give them to you for less than that." My grandfather put a crisp bill down on the counter and replied, "Here's $50. Thank you." And we walked out with them.

He was so secure in himself. He was the boss, a big shot. He'd walk around his fabric store and look at everything—the bolts of fabric, the drawers of buttons, the customers. He strutted about town the same way—scrutinizing and examining—as if he owned everyone and everything.

For the little girl in me who never wanted to take up too much space or be the center of attention, being with him was like being in the center of the sunlight. It burned, but it also glowed.

When I was with him as he commanded his way through life, I felt like I was somebody. When Grandpa walked into a store or a restaurant, people knew who he was. People both respected and feared him. He was a powerhouse, a force to be reckoned with. And the world was his oyster. Whatever the impossible was, he would figure out a way to make it happen.

When we were kids, Cabbage Patch dolls were at the peak of their popularity. You couldn't find one anywhere. But Grandpa managed to get four—one for each of his granddaughters.

He was most in his element at Sunday family dinners. Each week, he and my grandma would invite lots of people over to their house. Our group represented the entire Cuban-Jewish (or "Jewban," as we affectionately say) community in Montclair.

In his bright white guayabera, he would sit at the head of the table, which, for some reason I never knew, always had two plates stacked one atop the other. Always. That was the rule. It was our little Havana and it suited Grandpa's personality perfectly. After all, he had loved Cuba and soaked up the culture with gusto. Grandma and the other women would serve rice and beans or arroz con pollo. Glasses and plates clinked noisily. Everything was larger than life, like something out of a telenovela. People spoke Spanglish quickly, in voices that were loud and dramatic.

"Imagina ... el dueno de la otra tienda esta diciendo que toda la genta CAN hechar los caros IN OUR PARKING LOT! ¡Estoy tan enojado!"

After dinner, the women would clean up and the men would smoke cigars. Then they would go to another room and play poker. Very macho. Very Cuban. Very Grandpa.

If my grandfather lived his life in a kaleidoscope of color, my grandmother lived hers in black and white. As big and brassy as he was, she was petite and quiet. He took the world by storm. She ran for shelter.

My relationship with her was sacred. Her love was pure and unconditional. She would often say to me "If someone would come and say that Janie just robbed a bank, I would tell them she must have had a good reason." She was the one I could always count on, my go-to person. And yet, this beautiful woman felt practically invisible. "Janie, I was in Cuba for many years," she'd tell me. "If you weren't round and didn't have a big ass and curves, you were nothing. I was nothing there. No one would even look at me."

Her days and demeanor were filled with anxiety and fear. The sight of anyone in a uniform would take her back to her childhood in Europe and send fear through her entire body. She'd tell me about the Nazis taking her house to use as their headquarters and the time she went to swim practice one day when the coach said "Little Jew girl, you can't go in the pool anymore. You're dirty and we don't want to swim in filthy water."

That feeling of being dirty and having something fundamentally wrong with her stayed with my grandmother her whole life. It made it impossible for her to have any sense of self-worth or confidence in her value. It was even hard for her to accept how in love with her I was. I'd tell her she was my favorite person in the whole world and she'd say "Janie, I just can't believe that. I don't understand why."

They lived a few blocks away and we were together almost every day. No matter what we did, we were happy to be together. We could read or just be silent or watch television. When I was in high school, I worked at the fabric store in the afternoon. Grandma taught me the basics of business—billing, records, filing. We'd go out for lunch or go shopping and talk about everything. In her later years when she was ill and frail, sometimes I'd go over to her house after I put the kids to bed. I loved her spirit and how safe I felt with her. And when I buried her, I buried a piece of my soul.

I am relieved that she isn't here to see me sick again. I don't think she could take it, so in my dreams, I don't tell her. We chat and laugh, but my being sick is a secret. It is the only secret I have ever kept from her.

As close as Grandma and I were, it would turn out to be my grandfather's life force that would buoy me in the toughest times over these years. Although his bluster and brassiness made me cringe as a young girl, he also made me feel important and deserving. His if-you-want-something-you-take-it approach to life, that unabashed sense of entitlement and power and strength, all took root somewhere inside me.

As a sick adult, when I experienced those all-too-frequent moments of feeling like a nothing, a number, a body part, a disease, I would dig deep down and try to channel his essence. Invariably, Grandpa's spirit would lift me up and help me to move forward.

When I felt that I should apologize for being ill and needing so much from so many, I would try to reconnect with his feeling of being worthy and could almost hear him say "I am here. I hide from no one. I have needs. I have a big appetite. I have a big voice. I have big plans. I apologize for none of them and I deserve my place on this earth."

Mecca and the 52-minute lunch

In the spring of 2010, I entered what I called "the darkness." Once the insidious cancer cells had multiplied inside my body, I crept back into bed. For three months, I was either in a hospital room or in bed at home.

I was in a terrible place that I think most people would be embarrassed to admit to, where if I hadn't had my kids, I would have rather been dead. I simply didn't feel I could keep fighting for Round 2 of Jane vs. Cancer. Physically and emotionally, I felt as if this time it was more than I could handle. Also, I reasoned, I didn't want to be a burden to my husband and if something terrible were going to happen to me, I'd rather it be sooner than later. That way, at least he'd have a shot at having a full life with someone else.

We want to be independent. We want to carry our own bags. We want to clean up our own mess. And it's very hard to be in such a position of dependency when you have tried for many years to be self-reliant. I was great at supporting others —but *receiving* support from them? Not so great.

My friend John—always my rock and redeemer—was trying to comfort me. Nothing could lift my spirits.

He started grabbing at straws. "What would be something you could think of that is so wild and incredible that it would help you out of this pit?" John asked. "Something that you can't even imagine could really even happen—is there someone you'd want to meet? Something you'd want to do?"

Without skipping a beat, I answered, "I want to take Larry David out to lunch."

For me and millions of other neurotics, Larry David represents Mecca. Through *Seinfeld* and *Curb Your Enthusiasm*, he had exposed all of us in the most delicious way possible. Throughout the years of my various surgeries, procedures and countless days in a bed, when I couldn't focus, couldn't think, couldn't work, throughout all of it, Larry made me laugh. For a half hour at a time, I got to check out of Cancerville.

I had plenty of time to think—and had spent a lot of it daydreaming about what I would say to Larry if I met him. I would have imaginary conversations with him ... what I thought he should do on future *Curb* episodes and which one was the best.

John asked "Why don't you write him a letter?" Without hesitation, I replied "Why the hell would he care about my letter? Everybody's got cancer." "Janie, just write the letter," he instructed. And so I did.

July 31, 2011

Dear Mr. David,

I am a 42-year-old mother of two living in Montclair, New Jersey. The reason I am writing to you is that I am trying to accomplish my "bucket list," and taking you to lunch is on it.

I would like to meet and speak to the person responsible for some of the best laughs I have ever had. I have spent much time cringing in delight watching your show and also wondering how in G-d's name you come up with your stories. At the same time, I know I'm living pieces of it every day.

I will have scans in a few weeks to find out how I am responding to treatment for Stage 4 metastatic breast cancer. The doctors are hopeful that I can live a long time, but I'm not waiting for any more bad news.

Please accept my invitation to take you to lunch to continue down my bucket list. Actually, having lunch with you is the only thing on it. I would be happy to come to L.A. to meet you for lunch (my brother lives there and I would get to see him too).

In any event, I want to thank you for providing me with laughs and a little mental "time off" from what has been a really challenging time. I appreciate it so very much, and being able to thank you in person would be a dream come true for me.

Sincerely,
Jane Schwartzberg

I gave the letter to John. He knew someone who knew someone who knew someone. While waiting to hear back, I guess you could say I became a little obsessed—okay, maybe a lot obsessed. As I was trying to rehab myself—walking in the park for five minutes at a time—I started thinking about what I was going to wear when I had lunch with Larry David, whether I should have my hair down or in a pony tail and what we would talk about.

I prepared for the imaginary lunch with Larry that I was convinced would take place. I'll admit it was pathological. One day, I went to Nordstrom and told my favorite saleswoman, Cheryl, "I need to buy a beautiful dress for my lunch with Larry David." "Oooooh," she gushed, "When are you going?" "I'm not sure," I replied.

I bought a simple pink dress, brought it home and showed it to Mick: "This is the dress I'm going to wear to have lunch with Larry David." "You know," he said softly, "I'm really concerned about you. You've had a lot of disappointment this summer and I think it's great that you have something fun to think about, but you really need to be in reality."

"But it is reality," I said. "I imagine it and I see it. I walk in the park and I go over what I'm gonna say when he walks in. And all I need is for him to call me and I'll invite him to lunch." All I got back was an "uh-huh" with an implied but unspoken "Sure, Janie. Sure you will."

I knew my loved ones were just worried that my hopes would be crushed and that life was about to disappoint me once again. From my mother, I heard a sigh, "*Oy*, Janie, you with Larry!"

It was about two weeks later, when I was home talking to her on the phone, that I got call-waited. I saw it was a Los Angeles area code with an unfamiliar phone number. "Mom," I interrupted, "I gotta go. Larry is calling me." Then I quickly hung up, clicked the receiver and answered with a cheery "Hello?"

Jane!

Yes?

Hello, Jane.

Hello, Larry (like I knew him).

How ya' doing?

Well ...

Yeah, I heard, you're having a rough time.

We talked for about 20 minutes about the summer and lots of other things. When I sensed the conversation was winding down and he was about to get off the phone, I went for it.

Alright, Larry, you're about to hang up the phone, so I have to close the deal here. May I please come to L.A. and take you to lunch?

Absolutely, Jane!

How's Monday?

Monday looks pretty good.

Okay, Larry, I'm going to get on a plane and come have lunch with you.

Jane, I don't want you flying across the country. It's going to be a waste of your time to see me for 45 minutes.

First of all, my brother's there and I'm going to come visit him. Second, why do you say 45 minutes? Maybe you'll enjoy it and make it 52.

He laughed. Then he gave me his number and told me to call him Monday morning.

I just wanna be sure. I'm calling you Monday morning and we're having lunch on Monday.

That's right. I'll see you Monday.

I hung up and called my doctor to see if I was cleared to fly. "Weeell," he hesitated. Then I told him that I was going to take Larry David to lunch. He gave me the go-ahead. Well, I think he did, or if he told me I shouldn't go, I didn't hear him.

I called my brother to explain that I wanted to spend the weekend with him, and I was having lunch with Larry David on Monday. "Janie," he said, "just come to see me. Don't worry about this Larry David thing."

That was Wednesday. I had been in the hospital only a few days before. My incisions weren't completely dry. Fluid was still seeping from heavy bandages that needed to be changed every few hours.

I flew out the next day and spent the weekend with my brother. Then came Monday morning.

As I dialed the phone number Larry had given me, I was hoping and praying someone wouldn't answer "Joe's Pizza."

The outgoing recording said *"You've reached Larry David's office. Please leave a message."*

"This is Jane Schwartzberg. I'm supposed to have lunch with Larry today?" half telling, half asking.

A woman called me back a few minutes later and gave me the name of the restaurant.

Do you mind if he brings someone?

No. In fact, I still don't believe I'm having lunch with him.

Be there at 12:50.

1-2-5-0. Not 1-2-1-5. I had to make sure I heard it correctly. G-d forbid I am late for my lunch with Larry David.

Correct.

At long last, it was time to put on the pink dress that I'd imagined wearing to my lunch with Larry. My friend's sister had loaned me a gorgeous $6,000 Bottega Veneta bag to hold. It could barely fit a credit card but it sure looked fabulous. I put on shoes and make-up and I looked in the mirror and thought "Girl, you've got Stage 4 incurable cancer, but you are looking *good* for Larry David!"

I walked into the restaurant and it was just like I'd imagined. I told the maître d: "I'm here to have lunch with Larry David." She couldn't tell that I had just emerged from hell.

She told me that I looked beautiful and I responded "You have no idea how much I appreciate that."

And there I was, thinking: "I am so here. No matter what they tell me when I get back. No matter what the doctors say. No matter what the scans show, right now, I am the luckiest person walking this earth."

I sat down and a little while later, I heard shuffling. I looked up and saw *him*.

Jane!

Hi, Larry.

Nice to see you.

Oh my G-d, you're really here!

You're here. I'm here. We're going to sit and have lunch.

Not wanting to miss this once-in-a-lifetime opportunity, I blurted out*: In case anything happens … a fire starts, I pass out … I have to say, thank you, thank you for sharing your talent with all of us and with me, thank you for helping me get through these months and years, thank you for being exposed, and thank you so much for this moment which, no matter how long I'm here on earth, I promise I will never forget.*

Jane. I don't know what to say.

He introduced me to his producer, Laura, and we had a magical lunch.

We laughed and talked about healing and life and death and religion and everything, day-to-day life and all its craziness.

In the middle of lunch, I wondered how he was doing. After all, Larry was the basis for *Seinfeld's* George Costanza character, so I knew he was plagued by the all-pervasive Jewish neurosis about illness and death—something he'd mocked in the episode where Jerry, Elaine and George volunteer to be companions for the elderly ...

Ben: I feel great for 85 ... I'm not afraid of dying. I never think about it. I'm grateful for every moment I have.

George: How can you be grateful when you're so close to the end? When you know that any second—Poof! Bamm-O! It can all be over. I mean you're not stupid, you can read the handwriting on the wall.

Ben: I guess I just don't care.

George: What are you talking about? How can you sit there and look me in the eye and tell that me you're not worried?! Don't you have any sense?!! Don't you have a brain!? Are you so completely senile that you don't know what you're talking about anymore?!

So as I sat across the table from Larry, I was acutely aware that he might be uncomfortable since, I, like Ben, could be "so close to the end."

Larry, is it terrible? Are you okay with this?

No, it's actually quite pleasant.

He smiled. I got the sense he appreciated this awareness on my part and was glad I'd asked.

Before I knew it, we had finished eating. I figured I would say something to provide him with an exit strategy.

We're coming up to 48 minutes here.

I'm going to have tea.

Me, too (I was elated, thinking it couldn't be so bad if he was going to have tea).

I've kept up with Larry and Laura. They're cheering me on. I still can't believe it. I think about it every single day. I have been to Mecca and back.

Photo gallery

Mickey and me on our wedding day (October 31, 1999)

Mickey and me ... after the fall (2000)

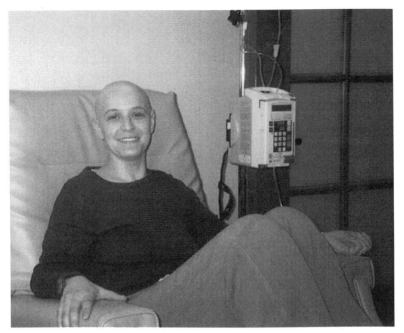

"Red devil" of a time (2000)

Mickey, me and "Elvis" (2000)

Our Vegas wedding menu

The wedding party: Mike, Toni, us, Greg, Sara

Mike and Toni

Mickey and Ally (2009)

Jack and me (2006)

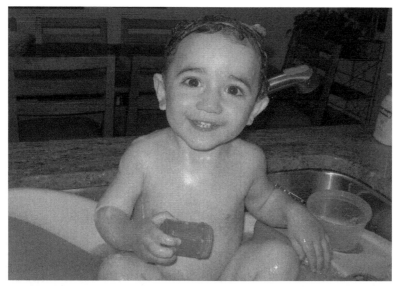

Jack (2006)

Ally (2007)

Snow White and the fireman (2009)

The parents (2011)

My sister, Sue, and her husband, Len, with Ben, Max, Gabe and Dash (2012)

My brother, David, with Mom and Dad in Cuba (2010)

Me and Mom (2013)

Grandma, Mom and Ally (2003)

Grandpa and Grandma (1990)

Bubbe and Zayde (1982)

Me with (clockwise) Janet, June and Lisa (1998)

John (2009)

Mickey and me (2013)

The family (2013)

Me in Mecca with Larry David (2011)

Love Train

If you were to ask me why I would like to be around for many more years, I would answer simply: I am really enjoying my ride on the Love Train. It's a term that was thought up by me and my dear friend Lisa, whom I call "Lisita."

The Love Train is the image we came up with to represent living our lives while very consciously and deliberately trying to spread goodness, share joy and elevate the people with whom we are on this crazy "ride." So we talk about "being on the Love Train"—and when we really feel like we're doing right by the world—*driving* it. We get to pick who comes on and we never run out of seats or feel crowded. Ironically, unlike the New York subway system, the more passengers there are, the more enjoyable the ride.

Lisa claims that when we met during our college years, I was not interested in being her friend. She has teased me for having to fight to get off my "B list." In my mind and heart, that could not be further from the truth. We met in a Jewish Ethics seminar at Columbia University, spring session of 1988. We were the only non-Orthodox Jews in the class. So whenever the teacher cracked a joke about a Talmudic interpretation, everyone would laugh but us. We bonded by feeling completely ignorant together.

Class ended and we pretty much went our separate ways until a few months later, when we were heading to the same engagement party and ran into each other on the subway platform. The memory of this casual encounter is embedded in my brain—unlike the names of the people who were getting married, which I couldn't tell you for all the money in the world. Lisa was wearing a fitted denim Ralph Lauren dress, looking so stylish and put together. I remember feeling like a *shlump* next to her. We talked for a bit and hopped on the train.

My friendship with Lisa didn't truly blossom until a couple of years later when we were both working on Wall Street, and it became one of the most important relationships in my life. I believe we have chemistry with our closest friends; together, Lisa and I are explosive.

The obvious people–like Mick, my folks, Sue and David—have always been with me on the Love Train. But I have been incredibly lucky to pick up the most remarkable people at stops along the way. Each passenger holds a little piece of my heart and history, as I feel honored to do for them.

I love to think about the time I met each one and how we grew to feel that organic, wondrous connection. For example, Jen and I played together when we were three years old because our mothers were friends. We've loved each other since we were little girls. She told me where babies came from long before my mother gave me the book *Where Did I Come From?* (Sorry, Mom. I didn't have the heart to tell you that I already knew.)

John is not *like* my brother, he *is* my brother. Since meeting through a mutual friend in college, we have never left one another's side. When the ride is smooth, we enjoy the scenery together. And when life derailed me, it was John who was instrumental in helping to get me back on track.

He's there for every doctor's appointment—and there are many. He guides me when there's a fork in the road. And he has never once let me down. The best way I can describe our relationship is to say that if there were a company set up for the sole purpose of giving me and my family an endless stream of unconditional love and support, this brother from another mother would be its CEO.

I am going to be honest about how, or rather why I met Mike in the courtyard at business school because I know my husband is (rightfully) very secure. I darted, and I mean *raced* (think O.J. Simpson in the old Hertz commercials running and hurdling over chairs through the airport) to get on Mike's scavenger hunt team during orientation because I thought he was really handsome. I learned that his Italian good looks were the least of his admirable qualities. Life is so unpredictable in the best way. I ended up in front of a priest in a church with Mike several years later—as the maid of honor to his wife, Toni. And I am able to ride my Love Train on many days because of their tender, steadfast support.

Susan hopped on the Love Train at my sister's wedding shower. We were sitting next to each other when I admired the toaster oven my sister had just unwrapped. We chatted a bit and I told her that dating was hell and that I didn't have confidence I would ever find Mr. Right. The next week, she sent me a brand new toaster oven with a note that read, "You don't have to get married to have a great toaster oven."

I met Joanne in the most boring class of all time: Cost Accounting. I fell in love with her humility and intellect as we discussed how to allocate the cost of electricity and rent to a company's products. We will never ever spend a day of our lives without loving each other. And that is despite the fact that she is a world-class athlete (no kidding!) and I have nothing going on in the fitness department. More than 20 years ago, after taking her regular marathon-like runs, she would walk with me just so we could talk. My big exercise for the day didn't even qualify as her "cool-down." She has been walking with me ever since.

Jim is a cancer survivor. He and Ginnie invested in my start-up company in 1998. The first time I got sick, Jim—my self-proclaimed "cancer concierge"—showed me the way through the morass of doctors, hospitals and treatments, while Ginnie held my hand.

Linda has been present at all of my major life events—my Bat Mitzvah, wedding, mastectomy, my daughter's baby naming and my son's *bris*. Although she started out as my mom's friend, we somehow developed our own sweet and lasting friendship. Now, I proudly share her as a friend with both my mom and my sister.

Wrapped in just a towel, I was truly Naked Jane the first time I saw Monica. She was a recent massage school graduate offering $20/hour budget appointments. My family and I were her first clients.

It was love at first sight the day I met June in 1993. Maybe it was because I told her my life story at the first meeting and she still wanted to be friends with me. I never could figure out why—she was so well-educated and cultured—but lucky for me, she did. I hoped that her crazy-smart twin sister, Janet, would ride the rails with us, too. And boy oh boy has she. In fact, she introduced John to his wife many years ago.

Although Greg and I did not really connect in graduate school, he would later become my adviser on how to run my company, as well as my confidante. Now he is a pillar in my life. Sometimes, sparks take a little bit of time to ignite.

Wayne, a contractor, came to do some fixes on our house in 2000. In addition to the ability to open all of our windows, I gained an incredible life force and friend. He introduced me to his girlfriend, Val, who in turn connected me to Karen. The three of us gals formed a love triangle of friendship that would extend even further, when Karen would be instrumental in helping me to keep a promise to my friend, Cynthia.

Cynthia could be a book unto herself. She was an amazing woman. Even though her electricity was turned off regularly, she constantly struggled to fill her fridge and she was battling chronic pain, she took in anyone who needed food to eat or a couch to crash on. I'd known her son for many years, but not well. He and I had gone to public school together since junior high.

Jamond, Cynthia's grandson, had lived with her since he was born. His parents loved him tremendously but she was in a much better position to take care of him. She watched over him like a hawk. She monitored whom he played with, corrected him if he didn't say "please" or "thank you" and made sure he was never, ever hungry. Instead of calling him "Jamond," she would always refer to him as "my Jamond."

When I met Cynthia, she had been battling cancer for a long time and Jamond was seven years old. Although from appearances we did not have much in common, we loved to be together. Sometimes, when I was with her, I would even feel the same wonderful way I did when I was with my grandma.

Cynthia understood that her time on earth was soon coming to an end. One afternoon when we were sitting on her small, cement porch, she confided in me that the only thing keeping her from letting go of this life peacefully was her concern for Jamond. She wondered how he would have a real shot at a full, productive life if she were not here to watch over him.

I didn't think twice before promising her that I would, along with his parents and other family members, see to it that Jamond had a chance. At the time, I had no concept of what a gift and challenge it would be to keep that promise. In fact, it turned out that I could not do it alone.

With deep sadness but relief for the end of her suffering, we memorialized Cynthia in a beautiful service and burial. With love, we turned to Jamond and the life he had in front of him. Friends and then their friends became a bridge for Jamond to a life without his beloved grandmother.

Almost everyone on the Love Train, and people related or in some way connected to them, helped me to keep my promise to Cynthia. Meals were provided. Jamond's teachers were engaged. Bicycles were bought, camps were paid for and rides were given when he missed the bus. It felt to me as if the entire world had shown up to show Jamond that he was loved. And he was.

And so our delicious and inspiring Love Train continues to chug along. Our lives are better for taking the ride together. We've introduced spouses and partners, helped one another get new jobs, supported chosen causes, buried loved ones, celebrated births and accomplishments, and simply listened to each other for hours upon hours. Together, we have helped one another to show up in our lives as best as we can, which really is the best gift ever. It is a tremendous privilege to share the ride with my fellow Love Train passengers.

All aboooooooard!

The agony & the agony

Cancer is a real pain. In fact, I can say with confidence that I know how to endure unimaginable amounts of physical misery.
I can properly strap myself onto an operating table, and I know that the moments before I am put to sleep for an operation will be the only opportunity I'll have to thank my entire surgical team for treating my body carefully and respectfully. I can navigate any big hospital and, if pressed, I am certain I could find a good vein and run my own IV line.

After the mastectomy and abdominal tram flap—where they pushed up my stomach muscles to create breasts—I experienced horrific, I-would-rather-be-dead levels of pain. So I made up a little game: Beat the (pain) clock.

I'd arbitrarily pick a short period of time and think to myself, for example, "I'm just gonna get through 15 seconds." I would say it to myself reaaaaaally slooooowly, to pass a few seconds. Then I would think, "Oh no, 15 is too long. Let me see if I can do eight."

Now comes the really exciting part. When I survived an increment of eight seconds, then I would bump it up. And I played the game long enough for a chunk of time to pass. Eventually, after distracting myself with this for 15 or 20 minutes, either the pain would have subsided an iota or it would be time for me to click for more morphine.

Since the pain game is a solitary endeavor, sometimes I couldn't play it. Just a few hours after my innards had been scrambled like an egg, who should walk in but Danny—one of the two matchmakers who set Mick and me up. For a good part of his life, Danny lived the life of an Orthodox Jew. A gay Orthodox Jew. Now there's a non sequitur if ever there were one. He was about as closeted as one could be, so much so that he got engaged to women three times.

But just before my first surgery, Danny had at long last connected with his authentic self and come out—with a vengeance.

He stood at the door of the hospital room, sashayed over to the bed and let out an exaggeratedly emotional "Oh my G-d, Jaaaanie!!" He went on, "Jaaaanie! Look at you! This is a mess! This is a disaaaaster!" He was unquestionably and fully connected to his feminine side.

If I hadn't just had massive abdominal surgery, I would have chuckled and been delighted for him. As it was, however, I had to hold on tightly to the cold bars of the hospital bed to brace myself. I couldn't laugh because I was stitched together so tightly that I was afraid I would literally split my sides. "Danny, please don't talk right now," I whispered. "You're just too gay for me."

A few years later, I had another opportunity to play the pain game. I was hospitalized for the VATS—video-assisted thoracoscopic surgery— the diagnostic procedure that revealed the cancer's reoccurrence. It's a fancy name for what is basically ramming a camera into your chest cavity so the surgeon knows where to cut out pieces of your lungs.

I was being prepped for surgery. I'd been shaved and covered with Betadine. I felt like an animal being prepared for slaughter. The nurse needed to start an IV line, but there was a lot of scar tissue around my collapsed veins from chemo. I told her she couldn't go in with the needle unless she was sure she had a vein. No poking around on the off chance she would find something. She went in anyway and came up empty.

"I will give you one more chance," I threatened. She was angry and looked at me with a face that asked "Who the hell do you think you are?" I told her that either I'd do it myself or they'd have to put me out and then run the line. She was nonchalant and didn't believe me. She jabbed in a new needle and used it to hunt around. Through gritted teeth, I said "Take it out." "No, I think I almost have it," she said. This time I screamed "Take it out!"

I got up off the gurney, confidently walked over to the nurse's station with my ass peeking out the back of the hospital gown and declared "She's not allowed near me. Not with a needle and not without a needle. And I want to talk to a doctor now. They have to put me out in the operating room and then run the line." And so they did.

When I woke up after the procedure, I felt the hard chest tube the doctor had inserted rattling inside me. It was attached to a softer tube that came out of my side and was connected to some kind of machine sitting on the floor, helping to inflate my lungs. After two or three days, they yanked it out, my screams notwithstanding.

It was hell. I was doped for the pain around the clock and when I went home I went through withdrawal. My heart was racing, my hands were shaking and I begged "Mick, help me, help me. I can't be in my body. My heart is going crazy." I paced around the house for hours, like an addict jonesing for a fix.

The pain of these surgeries still reverberates deep inside me on a sensory level. Even if I have to go to a hospital for a reason that's unrelated to my own body, the adrenaline floods my bloodstream, as if my body is expecting to be cut. I swear part of me thinks someone is going to come in and carry me off to another operating room.

When my son recently was in the emergency room, all the smells, the sights, the sounds took me back to when I was the patient. My body reacts as if it's hearing "They're coming for you." A dear friend of mine just had surgery. I couldn't visit her. I take a lot of passes. The people who understand that … I'll be friends with until the day I die.

Cancer bitch

I'll let you in on a dirty little secret. You just
have to promise not to tell anyone. We cancer
folks—sometimes, we're not that nice.

At the doctor's office, for example, we size up the
other patients in a sick, oncological one-
upmanship where worse ranks higher. You see,
there's a hierarchy in the cancer world.

It's similar to the side glance you might give to
someone else in a gym locker room—except with
cancer, it isn't about who is more muscular or
well-endowed. It's about who's balder, who's
thinner, and last but certainly not least, who's
sicker. In the poker game of cancer, it's like,
"Ha! You think you have it bad, first-timer?
You're an amateur. I'll see your cancer and raise
you one relapse!"

When a friend of mine told me her son had
lymphoma and that there was a 90–95% cure

rate, I said "I'm so sorry ..." And I was. But I was also thinking "I envy him. At least a cure is a possibility." If I had those odds, I'd be throwing a fucking party.

Statistics for women in my situation are dismal. Ask my mother. She's online 24/7 combing the sites for every nugget, every crumb on the disease. If you look at 10-year survival rates, only about 5% make it. There are lots of new medications, but no long-term stats on them.

The hope is that I am at the forefront of an exciting time in new treatment developments and that the current stats don't apply to me. But sometimes being on the cusp of a huge improvement in how long women survive and hopefully thrive is not always much comfort. When I read that they call the new drugs a success because they extend life by three months, well, it's very hard.

One of my doctors said "I have patients who are sick for years." That's what I'm hoping for: to be sick for years. Yay! Can you imagine? That's as good as it can get. Won't get better, but please don't get worse.

Meanwhile, I swear to you, he always brings up this Mrs. Goldberg who has outlived all expectations. I'm convinced she's the only patient he has who's completely defied the odds, and that is why he keeps mentioning her to me. My father says he hopes that one day the doctors will be telling people about Mrs. Schwartzberg.

.   .   .

Along with "please," "thank you" and "excuse me," there are many societal niceties we learn. Chief among them is how to feign interest when someone is speaking to you regarding something you could not care less about. I know that if someone is talking to me about something I'm not interested in, I should at least pretend to care. And if I feel angry or annoyed, I should check myself. The problem is, now that I am acutely aware that my clock is ticking, my buffers have slipped and all the rules have changed.

Let's say I'm at a party and there's that social sizing up of one another that people do, and someone starts a conversation by asking "So, what do you do for a living?" (Translation: Are you important enough for me to talk to?) Or maybe I'm chatting with women in the neighborhood and hear "What's the best school for my very gifted and talented child?" or "Have you tried the juice cleanse?"

I no longer have the patience or strength for the excruciatingly trivial or the verbal status check. And I no longer have the time. Literally.

I know the rules. Only now, I don't care. The pretending to be interested, I don't do that. I can't. After being so sick, my tolerance for minutiae is low. Many of the proprieties I learned in order to be a decent and social human being ... there's a point at which I simply refuse to engage and instead I turn inward.

Sometimes I will simply walk away. I may offer an "Excuse me" before doing so, but more often, I just leave. And I rarely go to parties anymore. It's hard to bear the small talk and the chit chat. To my ears, it is a painful cacophony of cackles and squeals.

I need tons of down time and often want to be left alone. I'm always reminding myself where my deck is stacked, that I'm sick, that I have an incurable illness. If something makes me feel bad, I need to get away from it and, conversely, if it makes me feel good, then I should try to prolong it. It's exhausting. I have a limited amount of RAM and need to ration it carefully.

· · ·

Even the doctors are not spared from my bitchiness. I remember getting a call from my oncologist in January of 2012: "I'm sorry to say you have a new spot on your lungs." I didn't hear anything he said after that, but I do remember vividly that, before I'd hung up the phone, I had made up my mind. The necklace would be mine—that very day.

I'd been eyeing it for over a year in our local jewelry store. It was simple—just a chain of hammered gold links. Given that I get a high from outlet shopping and am drawn to the clearance racks, my excitement over something so expensive took me by surprise. It cost more than I had any right to spend. But the smaller I felt, the more I wanted it. Something snapped inside me and reason flew out the window. That damn new spot gave me a free pass to make a frivolous and very expensive purchase.

I called Mick. "You know that necklace I've been admiring? I have to go to the hospital this afternoon and I would like to wear it to my appointment."

Then I called my friend who works at the jewelry store and said "It's Jane. Where's my necklace?" She told me it was displayed in the store window. I said "Well, pull it. I'll be there in a few minutes."

When I went to the hospital that afternoon, I took pictures of myself in a hospital gown wearing my new necklace. It was just as I'd imagined. The doctor had to push my 10 pounds of gold out of the way to examine my neck properly. There was no way I was going to take it off and make it easy for him. No, this was more than a necklace. It was a medal of honor that I'd fought for and deserved.

I lay there prone, like a cancer Cleopatra, with an air of entitlement and arrogance that could have landed me a spot on *The Real Housewives of New Jersey*. "That's right baby, that's right, you push that gold away," I thought. There certainly was no catwalk around the examination rooms, but in my head I was strutting like a Victoria's Secret model topped with attitude: "Uh huh, uh huh, *howdaya like me now?*"

. . .

Perhaps one reason cancer people can get nasty is because we're often in pain or terrified—or both. A few weeks after the diagnostic procedure that showed the cancer was back, I ventured out to run an errand. I was at a four-way stop. It was my turn to go, but when I accelerated, the car in front of me stopped. So I hit my brakes and was blocking a guy from getting across. He yelled at me and honked his horn. I rolled down the car window and screamed *"Go fuck yourself! I've got cancer!"* He looked horrified. He rolled up his window and drove away.

I never would've screamed at someone like that before I got sick. I consider myself a nice person, but Cancer Bitch doesn't give a shit. No one has ever called me that to my face. But I know.

Identity theft

When you spend a lot of time in hospitals, it's hard to recognize yourself. At least it was for me. Looking in the mirror, sometimes I would see a person in a hospital gown but not recognize her. I wasn't Jane, the woman who is loved and cared about. I was a number, a disease, a body in Room 323 with Stage 4 "mets to lungs."

It becomes increasingly difficult to connect with your essence and link to the person you were before you got sick. When who you are as a life force feels separate from your physical body, you end up feeling like just a bunch of organs. At least I sure did. I lost myself in layers of physical pain, emotional pain, medical bureaucracy, pills. I wore a hospital gown for what felt like an eternity. I reeked of Betadine and other antiseptics that wash away the germs but also washed away some of me. I knew no one working in the hospital really cared about who loved me, who I was, what I'd done. If I hadn't had a name on the plastic bracelet telling everyone—especially me—who I was, I might as well have been Jane Doe.

After the procedure that diagnosed the relapse, a visiting nurse came to help me at home. I had to sign a pile of papers saying, essentially, that I knew how grave my situation was and that I would not hold the nurse responsible for anything that happened to me. Her most important question to me, delivered in her beautiful Irish lilt, was "Have you evacuated?" "No," I answered.

After she asked me how I could look so pretty and full of life yet be so sick, I told my mom she had to leave immediately and wasn't allowed back. My mom walked her to the door.

When you're sick, it's down to the bare basics— your bodily functions. I was stripped of any attachment to beauty, sexiness, power. I checked my feelings of possibility at the door.

The next day the nurse called with an important question. "Have you evacuated?" "No," I told her and hung up.

The phone rang the following day. It was the nurse again. "I need it for my records, please tell me, have you evacuated?" she asked. "No, I haven't."

Two days later, my mother was in my bedroom, and we were sobbing together. The phone rang. My mother picked it up, and nodded while she listened intently and then turned to me. "She really needs to know." I took the phone and screamed "Yes, I have taken *a shit*." I hung up. My mom and I laughed together for the first time in weeks.

Anchors aweigh

When I was growing up, my parents had traditional roles—my mom doted on us and was often our class parent, while my dad earned a living as a corporate tax lawyer. Sue and I, and much later David, spent countless hours just a few blocks away at our grandparents' house.

It was a special treat for us to be able to do things there that we were not allowed to do at home. When we slept over, for example, we'd stay up really late playing cards. The next morning, bleary-eyed from lack of sleep, we'd be allowed to drink orange soda with our pancake breakfast. We'd laugh in sheer delight as Grandpa would deliberately scream out "Shit!" just to be mischievous. Then Grandma would get up, grab a bar of soap and pretend to wash his mouth out over the sink, all while we watched and giggled.

On Sundays, we would pile into the car to visit my father's parents, our Bubbe and Zayde, in their New York City apartment. Bubbe would make homemade French fries from potatoes sliced paper thin. As we approached their apartment door, we could smell the potatoes frying in the pan. She wanted them ready for us as soon as we walked in.

Then we would go to the Jewish deli in the bottom of their building. I knew that Bubbe loved watching me eat and I was eager to please—so even if I was stuffed to the gills, I'd finish my plate of turkey, mashed potatoes and *extra* gravy. It made her happy, and I was glad to oblige.

In my grandparents' New Jersey house, a mix of Spanish, English and even sometimes French was spoken. Grandma refused to speak German, because she said it held too many bad memories for her. In Bubbe and Zayde's apartment, I heard Yiddish and Spanish, and a little English. It wasn't until I was in high school that I realized some people in my family had an accent. For many years, I assumed everyone's family wove in and out of languages as they conversed and had come to this country from somewhere else. I was stunned in fifth grade when I learned that some of my friends' parents had actually been born in America.

After what my family had been through—traipsing across Europe, with the Nazis nipping at their heels—it's no surprise that my mom and dad tried to keep me safe by keeping me close. Early on, I learned to equate home and hearth with security.

All through elementary school and even in junior high, I didn't want to sleep at anyone else's house other than Grandma and Grandpa's. Whenever I attempted to, even if it was just a few blocks away from our house, I would end up calling my parents at around 11:00 p.m. to ask them to come take me home. My dad would show up half in pajamas, half in "real" clothes, to shuttle me back to the comfort and safety of my house. I felt a relief when I returned home, as if I had been away for years. There was a pang, a longing in my heart, to be safe at home with my mom and dad, sister and brother.

When I was 17, I incorrectly assumed that homesickness wouldn't be an issue since I was going to college only 12 miles from my house. I was wrong. For the first year and a half, practically every Friday, I took a subway from Morningside Heights to Port Authority and hopped on the #66 bus back to Montclair. Once the bus got through the Lincoln Tunnel and I knew I was close to home, I felt my whole body easing.

Although my parents had encouraged my independence, I was terrified of separating from them. I could not imagine how I would ever stand on my own, confidently and competently, without their constant presence and input. In college, I felt as if my life's anchor had lost all its weight and I was set loose to swim aimlessly and eventually drown.

After college, the anxiety dissipated to the point where I was able to go to graduate school in California and forget how bad it had all felt. That is, until decades later, when I found myself lying in a hospital bed after hearing that I was incurably sick. The same old terror washed over me like a tidal wave, and suddenly I was a little girl all over again, wanting to call my parents to pick me up from a friend's house.

At night in the hospital, I wept alone for hours, wondering if the illness was going to force me to say an early goodbye to those I loved most. I wanted my mom and dad to come rescue me and make it all better, as they had so many times before, and the fact that they couldn't was shocking—both to them and to me.

Eat, pray, eat: waiting for Godiva

Like most women, I've always had what I might call an "interesting" relationship with food. At times, it's been a weapon, a tool, a friend, a foe, a cure, a placebo, a con, a lifeline, a comfort, an obsession, an answer, a reason and an excuse. Makes me wonder who was consuming whom.

My appreciation for culinary delights, as well as my weight, have mirrored the ups and downs of my journey. Chemotherapy robbed me of my senses of smell and taste, along with any enjoyment of eating.

To assess my improvement as treatment started to recede in the rear-view mirror, I'd take out my stash of dark chocolate, both my nemesis and my best friend.

Day after day I'd try to inhale that delicious aroma which I could recall only vaguely but knew was still there—somewhere. I would take out a piece of chocolate from the box, slowly peel back the foil wrapper, bring it up to my nose and breathe in deeply, eagerly anticipating the smell of sweetness but coming up empty. I'd put the wrapper back on and put the chocolate down, knowing I would try again the next night. For months, I smelled nothing.

Finally, one day I peeled back the same foil wrapper I had taken off so many times and there it was—the confection of the gods. What a heavenly scent. I screamed "Mick! Mick! I smell my chocolate! It's back!"

I rewarded myself after chemo, joining my friends Mike and Toni and their family on a trip to Italy. It was a feast for the senses … I devoured the scenery, the sights and the smells. Ahhh. Italy's a good place to remember how to live.

Years later, after I was diagnosed again, there were two forces driving what I ate. The first was I had lost so much weight that I looked and felt weird. It seemed like I was walking around like Hester Prynne, only the scarlet letter on my chest was a "C." My doctor explained that I was wasting from "chronic disease." I didn't mind that for the first time in my adult life, my thighs did not rub together when I walked. I will admit that this was quite liberating and represented a whole new world—one with the clear absence of talcum powder and Lycra Spandex. However, it did not feel like "me."

The second force informing my eating was that everyone, including the press, was working hard to convince me that I could eat away my cancer. People gave me books describing, for example, how it was critical to stay away from sugar—the devil incarnate to be avoided at all costs; how strawberries would keep me from my early grave; and why shiitake mushrooms were so important for women with breast cancer. You name it and someone wrote that eating it would save—or take—my life.

So I ate ... and ate ... and ate some more. I ate nuts in the middle of the night. I ate avocados in everything. I drank homemade soup with turmeric, a supposed healer. I was told that I should be juicing ... although if I had, I wouldn't have been able to do anything else all day. I wondered who on earth had time for all this vegetable management.

When I couldn't force another piece of antioxidant-rich kale into my face, I started to eat cupcakes. I ate peanut butter ice cream because I wanted to look like myself again and, of course, because the peanuts were going to kill the cancer, decrease inflammation and reduce my pain. I poured olive oil on everything even if it bore no relation to anything on my plate. I stopped eating anything made with white flour and then would eat double because I was so mad at having spent a day without bread or pasta. If there was any shot that eating something in particular was going to help me or give me pleasure, well damn it, then I was going to scarf it down. And I did.

Our society's obsession with thinness has been a source of amusement over the years. People say such silly things. When I was at my nephew's *bris*, I was weak from the chemo and had to hold onto a chair for support. A woman approached me with a big smile and said "Janie, I know you've got cancer—but look at all the weight you've lost!" And when I mentioned to another woman that I was having trouble getting up the staircase, I heard "I know—but you look amazing!"

The celebration of my thinness was bizarre and disturbing, but it's moot now. I am happy to report that my thighs are inseparable friends once again.

Show 'n tell

My guess is that most parents find the question of what values they hope to instill in their babies much more challenging than how to get them out of the car. Not me.

When the kids were infants, I would start sweating from nervousness long before we reached our destination. The tram flap procedure—the one that had given me artificial breasts—had robbed me of abdominal strength, so I couldn't lift the baby seat out of the car—at least not with the weight of a baby in it. Feeling envious, I watched other moms with their babies safely ensconced in a bucket of straps pop their kids in and out of their cars.

Of course, my arms could accomplish lots of other important "mom things," like hugging them, giving them baths, wiping away their tears or soothing a boo-boo. But the mere thought of having to pick up a few groceries for dinner while taking care of the kids reduced me to tears and left me feeling utterly inadequate. In moments of total insecurity, I wondered if I had any right to have children given how little I could do for them physically.

Sometimes I found ways to work around my limitations. On many occasions, I asked startled strangers in parking lots if they could help me lift the car seat and my baby from the car and put them into the grocery cart. Other times, I would wait until a friend came to visit me at home. As if I had not given a thought to it before, I would casually ask if I could run out for a quick errand while she stayed home with the baby.

Feeling clear and confident about what I wanted our kids to learn was always much easier for me. It still is. First and foremost, I want them to feel loved past the moon and the stars and all the planets. That is the basis of everything else that I wish for them. There are also other important things they need to keep in mind that Mick and I have tried to show and tell them.

They don't need to be smarter or look better or weigh less or run faster than they do. The world we live in can be so crazy. It will have us believing that we should spend lots of time trying to look or act like someone else. I want them to feel confident that the way they are is exactly as they should be. I am hoping they won't feel as if they have to spend time and energy trying to be anyone else, because if they do, they may not be motivated to become a company president or a great teacher or a rebel who starts a revolution.

I want to show them how to be the best and most loyal friends they can possibly be, but never to put up with people who don't treat them well. What I am hoping is that they will find just a handful of people with whom they can share both the good times and the tough times.

When they find these people, they should treasure and honor these friends and never let them go. Sometimes, these friends will have bad days and Ally and Jack will be the ones to help them get through. Other times it will be my kids who need the support. These good friends will listen and hold their hands and tell them they are not alone. They will help them to feel safe when the world feels really big.

And speaking of the world feeling really big, I want to teach them that it actually is and isn't, all at the same time. I hope they always remember that no matter what, all of us really want the same thing: to feel safe and loved and to help make the people we care about feel safe and loved.

I want Ally and Jack to be prepared because people will say mean things to them when they don't like something about themselves. When I was in Mr. Gill's seventh grade class, I got up behind a podium to give a speech. I was so short that someone yelled "Stand up!" even though he knew I was already standing. I stood there for what felt like eternity waiting for everyone to stop laughing. It hurt my feelings, of course, but I gave the speech. I want my children to be inspired to give their own version of a speech even when they feel crushed by someone's actions or words.

Like all kids, sometimes Ally or Jack feel scared, especially at night. I try to remind them that there is nothing wrong with being scared and that when I was a little girl, I could not understand why there were so many strange and frightening things going on in the world. I don't want fear to stop them from going forward in their lives, seeing the world, and doing the most good they possibly can. I want to warn both of them that if they keep themselves from being adventurous, the world will feel too big to navigate. I want them to take planes and trains all over the world.

I hope the kids are never embarrassed or ashamed to ask for help. Over these past many years, I have had to ask for help many times. We all need help at different times in our lives. I have learned to think of it this way: Whenever we ask for help, we are giving those who love us an opportunity to lend a hand. When we are in a different or better place, it will be our turn to extend a hand to someone else. That is how the world works.

When they are older, I hope my kids will find worthwhile ways to spend their days, fulfill their passions and soothe their souls. And if they're really fortunate, someone will pay them to do what they love and their avocations will become their vocations. No matter what, Mick and I will be proud of them.

If they can do or give anything at all to help out someone else, I want them to know they should. Sometimes it's tough to figure out how to do this, because it's often a choice between taking care of ourselves and taking care of others. After many years, I have finally learned that it's impossible to take care of anyone else unless we are first taking great care of ourselves.

I want Ally and Jack to know that they can help out people and our world in many simple ways. Sometimes just showing others kindness is a way to improve the whole world. It could be with their brains or time or money—probably at different times in their lives it will be in different ways. But they have to figure this part out for themselves because it will help their hearts to feel full and will make them feel even happier to be on this earth.

Ally and Jack will make lots of mistakes along the way. I did too and still do all the time. One of the most precious things I would like to show them is to how to *forgive*—others, to be sure, but also *themselves*. I forgive myself *everything*—all the things I wish I'd done differently or better, things that other people knew about and things no one saw.

Above all, I hope Ally and Jack will show themselves constant kindness. I want them to have as much compassion for themselves as they do for the most deserving people in the world— because to Mick and me, that's who they are.

The waiting room

Several months after we found out that the
cancer had spread, I was barely functioning.
My family and I had another appointment to
go to, another waiting room to sit in and more
fearful anticipation of what we were going
to learn.

I was in a haze when we arrived at Sloan-
Kettering. As we walked to the elevators, I was
struck by how nice the place was. There was
artwork on the walls, beautiful wood paneling
and the floors were spotless. The ubiquitous
hand sanitizer dispensers were the only giveaway
that we were not in a lovely hotel lobby.

We got off the elevators, and I wanted to run.
My stomach hurt terribly when I heard the
receptionist ask "Your name, please."
"Jane Schwartzberg," I said confidently. Fake it
'til you make it, eh? I mustered a pageant-like,
Miss Congeniality tone of voice, secretly

wondering if maybe, just maybe, they would tell me that I'm not really sick if I said the right thing, smiled a certain way or even if I explained to them how much my friends and family wanted to keep me around. Of course, that fantasy lasted only a second. In fact, I had come to believe that this illness would permanently define and contain me, my spirit and my potential as a human being.

With dread, Mick, my parents and I approached the waiting area of the floor. As I looked up to find a seat, I saw some of my fellow Love Train passengers. The sight of them took my breath away. They had crazy, full lives and already had come to so many appointments with us. None of them had told me they would be there. Seeing them sitting there changed something in my brain.

I could not remember who I was outside of sickness, but I knew very well who they were. And if I could connect with the love they each had for me, then certainly I would be able to find my way back from being a disease to being Jane again. And on that day, because they showed up to sit with us, I slowly started to emerge from the darkness.

We waited for hours, mostly just sitting there quietly. The silence spoke for itself. They understood that the best thing they could do to support me was to do absolutely nothing but exist with me in my utter fear and uncertainty.

For some, this quiet place is almost too much. I get it, believe me. But my friends knew that just being with me was "doing," too. They sensed there was no need to fill the air with words or the time with actions simply because my situation is one that makes us exceedingly uncomfortable. They recognized that showing up in my world was an outrageous act of love and kindness. They had held me up over the years.

I looked around at my friends and was overcome with gratitude. I knew how I felt about them and that they cared deeply about me, but I would have given anything to know what they were thinking right then and there. I'd rather get inside their heads now than let others have that privilege one day at my funeral.

Of course, John was there—he was always there …

What a ride it's been, Janie. I remember years back when my fraternity brother introduced us because you were having trouble making friends in college. Pretty funny, considering you were like the mayor of Montclair and later at Stanford you would more than regain your mojo and become Naked Jane.

This whole journey began with a tiny, hard lump. You were probably at your healthiest, working out every day, a happy newlywed. It was like "Where did this come from?" And when you found out it was cancer, it was Mickey you were worried about and whether you'd be able to have children.

Some people have the idea "We're gonna beat this," and I know you outright reject such fanciful thinking. You always say you need to be in reality.

You're amazing, Janie. Not only are you talented, but you have a way about you—very direct, a velvet hammer, opinionated but not judgmental, and you speak in a way that makes people feel good, which is why they feel so comfortable talking to you about their problems. You're a great listener. People walk away wiser, with a better sense of what their problems are and what they can do to fix them.

I like to think you're gonna be around for a long time and that you'll enrich my life and the world for many years to come. I don't think too deeply about "what if?" The possibility is there, but my hope for you is much greater. That helps me to deal with it.

I always try to go to your doctor appointments and tests with you. Secretly, I have this idea that I can be a good luck charm. I try to be calm and offset the fear.

… and Lisita …

So much has happened since we first became friends. We were two of the few women analysts at investment banks back in 1990, and we'd work 150 hours a week. We'd meet for dinner on Saturday night—and then go back to work.

You're like a sister to me, my go-to person on important decisions in my life, the person whose judgment I value the most. You have an unbelievable combination of smarts. Obviously, you're extremely book smart, but that's not why everyone who meets you craves Jane time. You're so loving and authentic. You have an incredible pedigree, but you don't take yourself seriously.

I'm a better person because you are my friend. I have more empathy and am just amazed at the human spirit and what an individual can endure. I ask for your advice all the time and you always give me good counsel. I'm further along in my career, happier as a mom and wife, and in a better place generally because of you.

When you found out you had cancer again, you cried. Not for yourself, but for Mickey, your kids and your parents. You were worried about whether you were going to be around for Ally and Jack. I remember you said "We're all going to die, but how much of my children's lives am I going to see?" Even little Jack asked you "Who will take care of me if you're not here?"

There have been many happy times over the years. I like to think back on your wedding. You looked so magnificent, with your jet black hair and your beautiful white dress. You were already sick, but of course no one knew it.

We still laugh about the time I told you that barrettes are not a good style choice for a grown woman. You gave me credit for breaking you of that habit. And whenever there's a fashion decision to be made—like when I told you, Stage 4 cancer or no Stage 4 cancer, that hideous fanny pack had to go—we'll use the barrettes as a barometer of style missteps: Is it as bad as the barrettes?

When we went on a weekend trip with our daughters last year, there was an element that wasn't lost on me, that you want our girls to become friends. I hope they'll be friends for 30 years and we'll be watching them.

I know that you don't want to hear that everything is going to be okay, and you know how hard that is for me to keep it to myself, because I'm such a glass overflowing kind of person. I do believe a bit in positive fatalism and willing good things to happen, so I still think you're going to be here for a long time. Maybe it's just selfish.

... and Jen, my friend since childhood ...

Even in kindergarten, Janie, I knew you well. I remember when the lunch aide said you had to finish your milk before you could go out and play, and you told her you didn't want to drink any more. Looking at the warm carton of milk and back at you, I knew what lay ahead, even as a five-year-old, and I pleaded "Please don't make her drink the milk," and thought "Or you'll be sorry." Well, no dice. Down went the milk and up came everything.

There's always been fun and laughter with us, even in tough times. Just before your scheduled C-section with Ally, you couldn't bend, what with the baby and the plastic netting holding you together inside. And you said "Jen, I have to ask you a favor—can you help me shave my legs? I can't reach down." And as I put the shaving cream on your legs and started shaving, we laughed until we cried. I guess our humor is our gift to each other when things are difficult.

We've always been intertwined. You're the sister I never had. You know what makes you so remarkable? The way you're so genuine and down-to-earth, accessible and kind. You have every right to be pretentious, being Phi Beta Kappa and summa cum laude at Barnard College, going to Stanford Business School, but you're not.

The first time you got sick, you were determined to fight the good fight, and you did. Then, as time went by, you started living your life again. We had a big "thank G-d I'm okay today party," celebrating the 10-year mark. Then it came back. It was so hard. In those 10 years, you'd known people who had gotten sick a second time and passed away. Not that you didn't have a lot to lose the first time, but now you have Ally and Jack. Now, there's even more to lose.

Since the relapse, you've kind of softened. Not giving up the fight—not ever—but giving in to the new reality, the "new normal," as you and Mick call it. I know how much it annoys you when people say you're going to be fine. You're no Pollyanna. And when you're afraid and in a dark place, I just try to be with you, next to you, keeping you company in your feelings.

161

I try to be the one you can share anything with, even the scary stuff, and to be right there next to you and not afraid of your fear. It's scary for me, too, sometimes, to be the friend of someone who's facing so much. But it's what I want to do, to keep you company in that terror and all the ugly places. It's all I can really do, I guess. Just be there.

… and June, whom I've known since grad school …

I know denial isn't a "Jane place," but I am quite comfortable there, thank you very much. I feel pretty confident that one day when I'm 80 years old, I'll still be able to pick up the phone and talk to you.

One thing about you that draws people in is that you're unfailingly supportive. Unlike you, I'm very reserved and there are very few people I'll confide in, but you are most definitely one of them. You're the one I've called in the middle of the night and you've told me you'd have been angry if I hadn't. You have such patience. I know I'm not the only one who feels like this. It's so easy to fall in love with you.

Do I think there will be a cure and you'll never have to think about having cancer again? No, I think this is as good as it will get. I worry more that your life will be so stressful than I worry about death. Every pain, every ache, every bout of exhaustion, every flu becomes very scary and I don't think that's going to go away. You know more people who have died from cancer than any of us and you have buried a lot of friends. I think you draw energy from being able to be a source of support for others, but I also think it's wearing. You're the person in my life I pray for most.

... of course, Linda was there, too ...

I'm more than 20 years older than you. Our friendship really began when you first got sick. I remember being so impressed at how you took complete control, like it was a business problem. You were determined to fight this thing, make decisions and not look back.

For your big surgery, we all wanted to be part of your family's support system. All of us gathered in a big open area of the hospital. There were platters of deli sandwiches. Everyone knew it was going to be a long haul and they just brought

food in, because what good are we if we're not
eating? There we were, eating and talking—and
even cracking jokes!—never forgetting why we
were there, but trying to keep it all light and
breezy and as upbeat as possible for your
parents and new husband.

And now here we are. Fast-forward 10 years
and we all thought everything was okay. Then
you got whacked again and your psyche was
so damaged. We were mournful and also scared
for you when you took to bed. I said I'd come
over anytime and just sit on the bed with you
and you told me you just wanted to be alone in
a dark room.

It was okay. You're a fighter. You just needed to
do your wallowing. It's part of the process. Then,
as you came out of it, you gathered your strength
about you. And you have the best support system
on the planet, which is a reflection of you. If
anyone wanted to learn about you, all they'd have
to do is look at the people you have around you.

And whatever we do for you, we know you would
do the same for us. Even in your worst times,
you'd ask what was going on in my life. I'd tell

*you to forget it and that in the scheme of life, it
was unimportant. And you responded that no, it
was important. You always have time for other
people. For me, that's remarkable because I think
that, honestly, if I were in your shoes, I'd be
focused on me.*

… and last, but certainly not least, Karen …

*I'd known you were special since we met seven
years ago, when my young husband had a
stroke. I was really struggling at the time and
you were in a good place, pregnant with Jack.
It was just a convenience that we both had two-
year-olds. Our connection was instantaneous.
You understood.*

*I think because of your struggle with cancer, you
weren't going to toss out empty platitudes like
"Don't worry, everything will be okay." I know
other people meant well, but you really got it.
Funny, we were at a stage in life when people
don't make new friends easily. We could barely
keep up with the friends that we had. You helped
me so much.*

From the start, I knew I could trust you. How many hours did I sit in your kitchen, crying and talking, while the kids played nearby? We had really tough financial times back then and you helped in a way that didn't make me feel uncomfortable, like bringing over meals.

And who else but you would've promised a woman who was dying of cancer that you'd look out for her grandchild, Jamond, after she was gone? It took you years to get him into the system. He didn't even have a Social Security card. When it was more than one or two of us could handle, you recruited friends and organized a team to schedule play dates, organize camp activities and much more. We each fill different roles in Jamond's life. None of this would have taken place without you.

I know I can count on you for anything. There's no keeping track or worrying how I could ever repay you. I thank G-d for you, Jane. Every day.

Beshert my ass

If you want to really infuriate me, you'll tell me that this whole mess was *beshert*, Yiddish for "meant to be." You'll tell me "This is part of G-d's plan." It has to be okay one way or another and maybe it is in some crazy plan, but I promise you that these are the last things I want to hear from anyone.

Don't sugar-coat or try to put a positive spin on what's going on—in fact, it comforts me when you acknowledge that my situation stinks and that I am looking at a life far different from and likely much shorter than anything I ever imagined. I know these things are said with good intentions, but *please* don't tell me "I know it's all going to be okay," because you really don't.

My mother likes to fantasize. She sometimes says "I'm still hoping they'll say you don't have cancer," which bothers me terribly, because I do. There is no question. My friend Janet delivered packages with my tumor to Sloan- Kettering so it could be studied a second time. In those days, I hoped, hoped, hoped they would determine that someone had misread the slides and there had been no reoccurrence. But once I was given the definitive news, once I knew, I had to accept reality because being in denial will not allow me to fully face my situation.

People want to do something to help. So when they ask "What can I do?" I ask them to pray for me. Do I think someone is actually listening and will answer? Not really. I have faith only in the present—but I'm comforted tremendously by thinking of the people who are putting out positive, optimistic energy on my behalf.

I ask people to pray for me because I believe in the collective power of love and caring, and that all that really matters while we're here on earth is our connection to one another. Often I ask people to pray for me and to think of me strong and healthy. Because while I can't remember me that way, they can.

Prayer is a way they can feel like they're helping me, which they are, and it's a way for us to connect in love. My friend Brian sent me an e-mail after getting back from Rwanda and told me that he had stood with thousands of Rwandans and prayed for me. I broke down. Thank you, thank you, thank you.

I am lucky to have so much love in my life. There are many people who are rooting for me, and who have made clear they would like me to continue being on earth. And that's incredibly comforting.

A taste of terminal

My clock ticks loudly—louder than most. There is a sword hanging over me. And yet, I wish everyone could have a taste of terminal and feel as I do—just for a little while. I would like people to know what it's like to have incurable cancer without actually having it.

Because only when the clock is ticking loudly do you truly realize that every minute of life is worth fighting for. I know it sounds trite but it's true: Every day we are alive, we have to remind ourselves to love life.

Cancer has taken many things from me—most important, time and peace of mind. The veil of ignorance and innocence I'd worn until I was 31 was yanked away and there was no turning back.

Still, if there is anything positive to come out of this utterly miserable and ongoing experience, it's that while I live with fear and dread, there is also a nectar-like sweetness to my days that I fear many don't know. It's as if I have been let in on a secret, and it is simply this: All that really matters is the love we give and receive.

Yes, we are all going to die. Yes, we are all in some version of the waiting room. We just don't know how long we're going to be sitting there. There's the oft-heard "I could get hit by a bus." But there's no process with that. No separation. No apprehension. No introspection or anticipation.

Everyone is scared of getting what I have. The prospect of death is terrifying. We all try to distance ourselves from it. If we hear someone has lung cancer, we ask "Was he a smoker?" Or when someone young dies from an illness, we cling to "Maybe she got bad care from her doctors." We'll find anything to justify feeling as if another person's dire situation is not one we will have to face. But make no mistake about it, there often is no explanation. It can be completely arbitrary and random. That's what's so scary. Everyone is walking around with something. We all have a hole in our hearts, a weight on our shoulders, something that's dragging us down. And it doesn't have to be cancer or even a medical challenge. We suffer from different forms of heartbreak. In my mind, the challenge is not to avoid it. Rather, it's to get up again and walk tall, with an open heart—despite it.

Although on many days I function really well and feel a tremendous amount of joy, the truth is that I am petrified.

The bogeyman comes out at night. When everything is quiet, I am scared out of my mind. Sometimes, I go to the dark place, a web of anxiety and anticipation. In the middle of the night, when I am really in touch with my cold, harsh reality, I feel lonely—not from a lack of people or connection, but from the knowledge that we come into and go out of this world alone. And sometimes I am just really tired from fighting to be here.

We all know very clearly and openly what the possibilities are. In the absence of a cure, we will continue to treat. My loved ones and I set aside the statistics and believe in the possibility. We have to.

I've made promises. I promised my mother, for example, that I will outlive her—even if it's just by a day. I don't think she could bear being in the world after I'm gone. My father comes to me often, takes my hand and says "You're my little girl." I feel terrible about all the angst my illness has caused my family, especially my parents.

I think about when I truly was his little girl, and how I never caused him or my mom any trouble. I followed the rules and pretty much sailed through the public schools in the town where my parents and grandparents lived for more than 40 years.

In fact, I made it all the way to high school without incident. My good girl streak came to an end in my junior year, when I went to a party where I knew there'd be drinking. I didn't tell my parents I was going. They thought I was at a friend's house. Everyone else seemed to be lying to their parents and hiding what they were doing, so I gave it a shot. I actually didn't want to drink anything. I just wanted to hang out with the cool kids.

Our neighbor's son was rushed from the party to the hospital to have his stomach pumped after excessive drinking. When he sobered up and his parents asked who was at the party, he offered up my name, because I was the one person he was sure would give the event an air of nerdy acceptability.

His mom called mine to tell her what happened, and my mom explained that it couldn't have been me because I was at my girlfriend's house that night. When I told my parents the truth, they were stunned—and disappointed.

I promised myself I would never again cause them such stress. Then cancer got in the way and made me break that promise.

Today, I make only one promise—that I will show up for my life and loved ones in the best way I can. I find meaning and pleasure in things that, if I weren't in the situation I am, would be trivial. I find meaning in getting up and going to work. Or a great conversation. Or a perfect cappuccino. And isn't that how it should be for all of us? Find some joy whenever we can, wherever we are in life.

Even if you haven't had cancer, you have to fight to show up. Some times are easier than others ... to feel capable, to do well by those who are important to you, to take good care of those who rely on you—and to feel worthy.

There is a rabbinic teaching that every person should carry two pieces of paper, one in the right pocket and the other in the left. One piece should say "I am but dust and ashes." The other, "The world was created for me."

These seemingly contradictory truths are equally important to carry in our figurative pockets as we move through life. The trick is to hold them both close. We are nothing in the world, and we are everything.

When life goes our way and we're feeling a little too secure and self-important, it's good to remind ourselves that we are a tiny speck in the universe. And when life hands us disappointment, as it inevitably will, we need to know that the whole world was created for the potential we hold.

Each of us has an opportunity to contribute to the world in our own way. But we have to balance feeling secure with the awareness that we are largely powerless.

I was moved by the way Rabbi Jeffrey Summit of Tufts University's Hillel explained the significance of the teaching: "We're human and the goal is not to do everything perfectly right, it's to continue to be in the game, to keep figuring out how to put our precious time into things that really matter ... and to know when to pull what message out of which pocket."

My latest scans show the cancer is stable, thanks to an oral treatment I recently started. Luckily for me, there are new drugs being approved all the time and more are in the pipeline. When this one doesn't work, I will try another. I hold out hope. I want to change the world. How can I do that if I'm nothing against the cancer? I have to believe I matter and that I have a right to be here.

I am my grandmother and my grandfather—one who believed she was nothing and the other who knew he was everything. There will always be a

part of me that feels small like Grandma, but it's
Grandpa who helps me to keep fighting.

I am but dust and ashes. The world was created
for me.

Made in the USA
San Bernardino, CA
16 September 2013